Mother
Daughter
Bond

Mother Daughter Bond

Something that Lasts Forever

Roshaunda Alexander

Library of Congress Control Number: 2015915725

ISBN-13:

978-1-952405-94-5   [Paperback Edition]

978-1-952405-93-8   [eBook Edition]

Printed and bound in The United States of America.

Published by

The Mulberry Books, LLC.

8330 E Quincy Avenue,

Denver CO 80237

www.themulberrybooks.com

CONTENTS

Over the years

what you *teach* me

just between us

A daughter is
a little girl who grows
up to be a friend.
—Unknown

FIVE STAR®
★ ★ ★ ★ ★

Why I'm proud of you

*A daughter is
a gift of love.
—Unknown*

What I feel for you

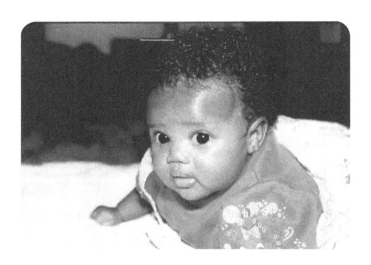

To my beautiful daughter, Ameerah Bilil—a gift from the Creator!

I always did my best to protect you and still do!

Definitions

Mother—female parent source: gives birth to cherish, to protect

Daughter—Human life female offspring

Bond—band fetters: uniting strong force: obligation cause to adhere

EQUAL

Happiness: a real, true friend for life!

Deep, Deep Dedication

To my parents, Thaddis Alexander and Shirley Alexander.

May you two rest in peace and always remain close to my heart.

♥   ♥
Forever
Young

Acknowledgments

First off, I have to give and express and glorify the Most High, the Creator, for giving me the gift to connect with words and thoughts and express them in many, many forms on paper! Pens, pencils, papers, and erasers have always been the given tools to me from the Creator. This is a way of soothing me and calming me down. Thank you, Lord.

I also thank my mom and dad for staying together as a strong unit. I tell you—had I not seen you two as my first powerful and loving couple, I would be lost today in the world I live in every day! Thank you both for always being there for me.

And to my spiritual mom, Dolly Smalley, who will always be my ommie—thanks so much for discovering I was a straight-born writer who can really do nothing else for too long. You always knew my sanity was connected to writing beautiful words. Thanks, Mom!

And extra-special thanks go to my second-grade teacher at Normandie Avenue Elementary. Mrs. Wagner, you cared about me from day 1. I will always remember you and my kindergarten teacher Mrs. Rogers. I have never forgotten all those caring words you shared with me. Thanks for being my first real public-school teacher. Love you always.

And yes, angels are real and have always been real in my life. I thank all my angels that stayed around and the ones still around me, still guiding and protecting me. I couldn't have made it in this world without having angels on my side.

Special thanks go to my sister, Wanda Alexander, for teaching me how to never let the wild side in me die. Thanks also to my homeboy Brian from around the way. I hope you didn't give up on me. You were always there and still are to keep me motivated. And special thanks to Ice Cube, my favorite rapper. Thanks for allowing me to meet you on the movie production on first Sunday and for my being featured next to you when you walked out of the church. Dancing next to you at the end of the movie made me famous. A lot of loved ones always share about seeing me next to you. Thanks from one of your number 1 fans.

Mrs. Pullium, I thank you so, so dearly for all the love and help and support you showed me. Thank you for passing the torch and for showing me and sharing all that extra wisdom of what womanhood is all about. Thank you.

And at last, my divine close, close energy. Thank you for really, really helping me stand strong on these legs and guiding and showing me how to keep going when the going gets tough. Thank you, thank you. You know who you are. I hope you are proud of me.

And to all that I may not have mentioned—trust me, you are all so dear to me. As I write, all of you are in my heart as well.

Peace and much, much love,
Queen Roshaunda

Let's travel into the world of deep talk and deep thinking!

Butterfly love never too quick to land.

We can do it—just do it!
Long as you stay out of our way,
we won't overthrow you.
Mother-daughter bond!

Quote By
Queen Roshaunda

Introduction to the Power of the Mother-Daughter Bond

Hello, beautiful readers. For the first time, let's give notice and become very well acquainted to what I call the power of a mother-daughter bond. A mother-daughter bond is a strength of pure, real closeness given comparison. It is almost like tying shoelaces, a cord, or string for tying fine net—tied so tight it is almost impossible for the strings to come loose! When a mother knows the power that she has with a daughter, she can assist and help her daughter in many, many divine ways for one simple reason. You have that trust from your daughter, so therefore, that is the pure connection you have from "the power of a mother-daughter bond."

I am going to define *pure* as "free of foreign-matter contamination, or corruption." If a mother does not know her pureness of connection of power in her mother-daughter relationship bond, welcome to a world of contamination from within and from the outside world as well. Being without is defined lacking, not having, unable to attain, and not having standing grounds, which is why it is most certainly not good grounds for a mother not to know the power of having that mother-daughter bond! However, I must say it. There are mothers out in the world today who really don't know the power of a mother-daughter relationship bond, and there are some that do—and you can always tell the difference between the two!

I am going to speak on it as clear as a crystal ball. A mother that knows the power in her mother-daughter bond, she is not going to communicate negative conversations about her daughter and spread her default in a negative tear down way. It's not going to happen, and the same goes for a daughter who knows the power of her bond with her mother. Her duties are to help her mother overcome frustrating battles of loss. Also, the daughter will not turn to using bad behavior to tear and take her mother down. It's just not going to happen between the two when their bond is pure and not contaminated.

The power of the mother-daughter relationship is respect! The mother respects her daughter as a daughter, and the daughter respects her mother as a mother. Let's be real. No one or no relationship can go anywhere right without that key ingredient of substance and respect! The power of a mother and daughter together builds up, not tears down. When a mother sees that discussion is needed, she brings it on. However, she only does it in a right manner or fashion, for she knows her daughter will know that her mother is only speaking in a way to help her, not in any way of trying to break her down. It is only to help her because the power of that mother-daughter bond is woven and connected the right way.

Now in some situations, at times, the daughter will humble herself first always and bring help of need that her mom may need. However, the daughter does as a daughter would, and that power from both of them knows not to start a competition striving I am out to do you, or win over you, or feeling as if I am one up over you.

The power of a mother-daughter bond knows what fake friends do, it is not a real bond and is no way more creditable of esteem or praise than what's sent from a divine connection, the Creator. It is always very important that a mother protect that bond with her daughter in a strong manner at all times at a very high degree. When your daughter is at a young age, this is the time when others whom you may not know who don't have good care, or concern, about your happiness and success of your life will for sure that there is entrance for room to come right in and start detaching that power of that bond. Don't become or be in a denial state of rejection this request; this validity of statement I am making will help you remain in strong, clear reality in a high regard as to ownership of this power of a mother-daughter bond. Therefore, nothing of wrong focus or wrong intent or bad behavior will be able to bend this bond. A wrong element, or wrong force, will have to go elsewhere because the two powerful force fields of a mother and daughter will cause all those of ill will to go on just because of the strength of that bond. Remember, what's real only does one thing to what's not real—that which is fake will be exposed. Remember, something discreditable feels ashamed and not wanted when bright light beams through it; therefore, develop and keep developing that bond and keep what's not good out.

I have interviewed a high percentage of mothers who did not know their power of bond with their daughter from not watching at close range, having one eye open when both should have been wide open caused serious division and disagreement to enter that realm of their bond now that wholeness of trust is not present. All that's present now is delusion, false belief that everything is okay nothing ever happen, now wrong just sits in and lots and lots of arguing goes on sometime for know giving reasons dispute with all use of file words, very sad all because of not knowing the power of mother-daughter bond and not being a gatekeeper at protecting that powerful bond.

Most of the time, the daughter really does blame her mother if bad unwanted situations occur in her life because deep from that inner being, that inner core of self, a daughter knows when she is a child, her mother is supposed to watch her closely. If a mother is not at fault, a daughter will know as well. You have to be aware that people can see well when something has power and is in the process of being and becoming better. You have to stay aware that there are a lot of humans in the world today, and some are very envious with resentful awareness, very jealous of advantage and seriously out to destroy a mother-daughter bond if given the chance to do so. Stand up for that bond; it's well worth it. Protect your power. Let no one come in and steal it. Don't allow the robber, the thief, to snatch what's given by the Creator.

When a mother and daughter are mentally aware together, very conscious of what their bond together is, and how to behave in that bond, they can do a lot of great things together, as well as help others and not be taken advantage of at the same time. There is so much help and work that can be done in this world we live in every day; however, in order to be consistent beings steady at different task, knowing how to use your power is of very much importance as well as being able to operate in the power of a mother-daughter bond.

It takes a lot of strong dedication for a mom and daughter to know how to move out into the world together and take it on. You have to be developed in having thickness and firmness in high regards to what must be done and accomplished. Having that energy of unity will be well seen some will try to take it on to try to challenge and dispute this powerful force when in the realm of unity, you just have to remain and stay strong enough to stand your ground on behalf of what you truly know is right and, most certainly, what a mother and daughter believe in.

Become very watchful of different invites that might be introduced to you. Some just want you around to start up havoc and confusion to take the extra effort at seeing how to get in to twist and confuse your right way of bonding. If a mom and daughter's bond is already glued the right way and has been interwoven from the beginning and there is daily development, meaning divine protection is around it, being able to see confusion and the games played by bad or wrong invites, That is not in best of intrance of attending any way. Clarity, clarity will not be the problem you will come to the conclusion it's just best not to attend.

Remember bad bonding is not a good thing. It is very dangerous, and it can lead you down the wrong path in life. It can cause so many poor, bad choices in life. All in the name of we bond it first, then I went ahead and accepted what was wrong for my life myself. This is why all invites are just not good for a mother and daughter. Stay in the knowing of your power that has been given to you in a divine fashion; this will show you the use of being sharp in areas of discernment, which are very important. Know that bad bonding is just not good. It is a bad power of its own if you give it your power of good bonding.

Mother and daughter, stay in your divine power of bonding into a right way of thinking and a right conduction of manners. There have been so many women, generation after generation, who may have already had a daughter or, in some cases, their daughters met a man that was viewed as their Prince Charming or knight in shining armor, that was thought of being anyway, however to find out just a manipulation. Many may even have married into manipulation. Nevertheless, not knowing the wolf in sheep's clothing had a wicked plan every day in that household who brought in division, confusion, serious start up of repeated drama, all in order of turning the mother-daughter bond into a nightmare of problems, confusion, disunity, and using all mission at hand to keep that real mother-daughter bonding of power from coming into as full bloom of season!

I wonder why. Could it be one of not knowing all along this bond of such high self-esteem could expose what's wrong that may or should not have entered in anyway? Be careful, become watchful—no one really wants to feel as if they're being played, or have been played. It can be done and will be done if they thought that there is a possibility of getting away with it. Yes, some do get played generation after generation—and more and more to come. This can be stopped only and if you have the knowledge at knowing and seeing what's going on.

Let me give you an example of this type of situation if it is not exposed in the beginning. Make room in your mind to hear what I am communicating from doing hard research under the titles *husband, boyfriend, close ones,* or *significant others.* Labels are just names, and some people hide under labels and titles to come in and break down a mother-daughter bond just to start having intercourse—yes, sex!—with your daughter and daughters. Sometimes, not always when older, it can start at a very young age. That is why you have to know the power of a mother-daughter bond. Bottom line: mothers, don't sell your daughter or daughters out for a reality of hell, case in point.

It is good to let the power of knowing how to live nobility: a quality state of being noble a reality of what's sane being mentally healthy. The more the power of mother-daughter bond is practiced, you gain a skill behind its energy. It is just like any other skill that you master. You become good at knowing what you are doing and winning at what you have practiced all in knowing what you're doing—and from this stance, power can be executed and carried out, fully enforced.

The power of a mother-and-daughter bond carries out so many different duties of high responsibility there's a lot of quick to respond different tasks that have to be performed and sometime real quick, but very calculated, which is why you don't need anyone no one around trying to destroy or bring that bond down to a low state, nothing worse than having a bad bond representation of a sign of no quality or no character. The light switch must be kept on at all times, the meaning as to what's being shared having understanding as to what's being done. In order to move around quickly and accurately, you must be connected right to having power in motion, and that can only exist from doing something right. Most people can relate to what happens. When doing wrong things, you remain at zero. The outcome is no power—which equals nothing manifested, totally powerless.

Always watch this bond very closely at real close range. I'd love to give you a beautiful example of the power of a mother-daughter bond. The president's wife, Mrs. Michelle Obama—she looks and acts so beautiful when arriving. And when you see her with both of her daughters, her daughters are beautiful, clean, intelligent, smart, and very well trained with high acuteness. Of all these qualities I have named, most would have to agree that all these traits are true when you see First Lady Michelle Obama with her beautiful daughters Sasha and Malia. However, under everything I have just mentioned, what you are witnessing/seeing take place is the power of a mother who bonds the correct and right way every day with her beautiful and smart daughters. The world should be so grateful and have high regards of respect to see what's shown for our eyes nationwide. The power of the unseen showed 3-D close-ups as we watched and viewed this real beautiful bond. Thanks, Mrs. First Lady Michelle Obama.

One important way of bonding with a daughter is to always read to your daughter. Even as your daughter grows up, you can step it up yourself from a different perspective of a way that's different when you read to a five-year-old. However, reading to your daughter when older is still good and important for the protection of your bond. It's a good way to connect with positive communication. Mother-and-daughter communication is extremely important. It's good sometimes to read out to your daughter, as well as it's just as great for your daughter to read out loud to you. It's a good way of seeing if those listening skills are up to par, which is very, very important just because of the society we live in today. We have to listen a great deal most of the time to operate correctly in the world, so for the reason being it's power for a mother and daughter to read to each other.

Let's have a discussion about the joy of the power of the mother-daughter bond. All the happiness, the laughter, in its unique way, is like nothing else. The feeling of happiness and being joyous—yes, this special surprise wrapped up like a special present on Christmas Day is all wrapped up in the joy of the mother-daughter bond, like sitting down eating a slice of delicious chocolate cake with a tall glass of organic milk. What a joy—it is so much fun sitting down, just enjoying away with your daughter so much divine-giving joy, talking, sharing laughter . . . so much fun with silly giggles, all in a silly manner of joy. Yes, you can have this fun of excitement with your daughter and your mom as well.

Just think back to your school days. Most of us from the female gender had a best friend at school, or lots of girls we were sitting around with on those bleachers while having so much fun with the girls. We ran always with extra excitement to meet up with our buddies. That same excitement can be transferred to your daughter with joy and lots of discipline, only because this is the mother-daughter bond that can't be mistaken for anything else but a mother-daughter bond. You will experience the excitement of joy within the bond. Remember power must be executed every day, carried out fully enforced the right way, but in a very good, determined way as well.

I can remember one day seeing a beautiful black dresser on someone's grass in my living area one night looking at that dresser sharing within myself that it was coming home with me. I walked back to my house and informed my daughter about it. At the time, we both knew that she needed it—a larger dresser. She shared, "Mom, let's go get it," and that's what we did. Somehow, with our two strong-willed minds used together, we did bring that dresser into our home. We cleaned it up, painted it well, and redesigned it. She liked it so much, and the dresser now sits pretty in her room. That was a positive expression of what a mother-daughter bond does: knowing when to take action when we need it and just doing it without doubt.

Devotion has lots of loyalty and dedication as to what's being, and practicing, faithful quality is something a mother-daughter bond share as well. Be honest about what is done when away from the home, letting each other know what's taking place so each can play her part, knowing what needs to be done and not allowing the outside world to defeat you at taking you out of your own element, just being able to perform all the tasks and duties that you must and most certainly will accomplish. Even when a mother and daughter are not around each other, their bond of power is still respected, just because of that divine respect for each another at knowing the high expectation of making sure that business is being conducted and taken care of. Therefore, the power of loyalty and trust is present as well.

Relationships are what I like to call ships that can sail out in many different areas out in the deep waters. It's all in the manner of how you respect your ship. Sometimes you may go way out into deep waters, sometimes the shallow sails, as I like to refer to when there is time for just rest, no talk. But you just have to define and be very clear as to what kind of relationship you're in and what it's supposed to produce for you and what you are supposed to do in it and thinking probably is of great importance.

A mother-daughter bond is a powerful relationship for this reason. This is why knowing how to operate and move out from it in the right way, there must be given accurate knowledge of how you manage it. Otherwise, abuse and wrong behavior can take their seats in it, just like all other relationships people take part and participate in, finding themselves not being able to produce that strong vibe of happiness. The power of a mother-daughter bond gives off so much self-assurance showing the world confidence, assuring that, in life, you have to keep punching. Giving up is not a good way of life simply because when one does decide to give up, you will have to stop using your force of a strong punch.

A mother and daughter in a powerful bond both know that there is just no room in their minds for giving up and to stop punching for this reason. If you stop punching, that means you're going to get punched on in many, many ways. You have to be really prepared every day in your life to not allow such behavior. You have to stay watchful when you're operating in the bond of power. So many seem to be watching it, however, trying to give an illusion or misleading visual image as to not being an onlooker. However, facts show that most really do watch close, paying attention. Remember some do look for that entrance, for that slip to prey on weak areas. However, really, these areas are progress in developmental stages. For some reason, people who think negatively and operate and think in a dark mental realm most of the time will try to take advantage of what they are seeing as a weakness if it can be gotten away with. I call these kinds of people mental bullies and mental cowards. Any power someone attains or have worked for—any connection in their seat of their own power—mental cowards will practice envy. So much which only produce a motion to come right in and tear that structured bond right down if given the opportunity to do so at any given favorable time.

A real mother-daughter bond represents structure, like a building arrangement of different elements. It's not a weak force; it's something that you must take the time and put extra effort at building at it so no one can tear it down. It will tear you down and expose your foolish behavior at the same time as well, so just stop trying to destroy what's been put and built from a divine mental plane. Its existence is real—a state of actual being, living in the now—the presence not afraid of dealing with all punches and blows that may come at you when you're alive and awake. This is why existence keeps foolish play right outside in the doghouse, if you get what I am saying. Way off in an exit like an expressway.

Remember struggle sometimes can be a very strenuous effort, overcoming lots of adversaries. This is why it takes a lot of great effort to operate in realms of intense competition for superiority. Just face it. Accept that people are always competing, and some just compete to see just if there is some strange chance at bringing your bond of existence to zero. Don't be surprised what I am sharing right now. Some people that you may know really don't care about you and really are just around your bond to see how it can be broken, just to walk away with a strong laugh, not giving a care in the world at how hard you may have worked to build it. Case in point: don't care!

Some might care to ask what's so different about a mother and daughter than bonding with a best friend. The difference between the two is that a mother-daughter bond, if built properly, moves in right conduct, taking care of business in a way that's not in being in competition with one another, because the glue that keeps the bond strong has been built to help not tear down or take each other into one-on-one confusion. Sometimes in friendship bonding, there can sometimes be more of a sneaky bond. Hopefully, it's real friendship.

I was always told by my father: "If you find one friend, you are very fortunate and lucky." I found this statement to be extremely true. So you see, the friendship bond holds more tricks in it, in a lot of ways. A mother-daughter bond exposes those who say that they're your friend or are just acting as if they want to be your friend.

Sometimes in those so-called friendships, a lot of valued time can really be wasted—whereas in the power of a mother-daughter bond, paying close attention shows that there is just no time to waste. Wasting your time is of no value. You have things to get done. Take care of all in the name of this power of bond knowing every day you must be well responsible and accountable for your own life.

A strong mother knows this, and her job is to instill this concept so much into her daughter's mind. If it takes of repeating over and over, this is what a mother does. Sometime people think a mother is nagging when sharing something over and over. That's not the case. In some situations, the mother has to make sure what's being shared has registered and gotten through so she then can move on to her next assignment, because a real mom knows that there is more information in time to speak on. The daughter's job is to take in all this valuable information of worth, process it, and go about to bring her positive desirability in her reality of want.

The mom must show that she has a strong conscious impulse; having it the right way produces respect between the mother and daughter. Conscious impulse will take you far, far into what to do right now—and also when given opportune, suitable situations that must be taken care of in a timely manner. Right impulse behavior moves in its right way. The opposite side to moving unconsciously in impulse behavior can be very dangerous just because of your acting on impulse but not having any conscious behavior. This type of conduct you do not want; that is for sure.

A mother-daughter bond holds a lot of high quality; however, both have to know when to swing up and when to block down. Otherwise, your discernment power will be in a tilt. When I say tilt your degree of staying focused in a steady consistent motion won't be a focused as up to part. Know that a powerful bond makes it all happen in the right and correct way, its power is just that. All your deeds of action will be in its proper alignment; you both will move around in the power of manifestation.

It's so great to know what you have as well as make demanding effort to protect it. This will help you in so many ways of not allowing anyone to come in to take, or steal what's of yours. Outsiders can always tell something that's built of strength and having the courage to know what belongs to you. Weakness looks a certain way and gives off a certain vibe, as well as strength. You can right off always tell something that's of strong honor and character. Remember, being weak is a deficiency in vigor of mind or character. This is why a percentage of people sometime who may have more than you will come off as thinking that you are less for not having, or exerting authority the way their view of you should be or what should have. Don't let these types of individuals' mind-set worry you too much, because your weapon that you use to do battle with in knowledge is living in the now of knowing—knowing what to say and do at all times and in any given situation.

A mother-daughter bond knows its power of how it is important to know what you do have ownership of and having that firm grip of holding on to what's yours and what you have to do to make all things and situations better. Knowledge is very powerful when carried out in an action plan. When something is not carried out, or demonstrated and seen from a clear perspective, you are not going to be taken as seriously as you should be. So take your mother-daughter relationship seriously. This will not allow others to just come in and step on your divine bond, as if they're walking on a floor mat. Staying in the knowing of awareness will stop all this foolish behavior of nonsense words and movement of no actions just because a lot of times, some people get very intimidated and fearful of what can't be torn down. It is sad, but this statement holds so much truth. Keep intrusions out, don't let what's of no good affect your powerful bond. In doing so you will be able to keep moving on forward and this is going to increase the likelihood of making progress. Progress produces a motion of self-worth. A mother knows how to help her daughter, or daughters, know why keeping your self-worth motion is very important.

The power of a mother-daughter bond gives off a feeling of accomplishment every day when operating in the power of this motion. The power of this bond makes you become very assertive. You know there could come a time when you both just might have to stand in assertiveness, to defend each other in all matters. Although a mother shares a strong bond with her daughter, both are still individually owned of themselves, which means knowing how to keep away from confused mental entanglements. This confusion only enters when a mother and daughter have no high regard for their bond and have high levels of arguments, and disputes with disagreeing words that take over their bond. This disturbing behavior will call for bad and wrong behavior, which will only hinder and hold back with regard to right discussion.

The high quality, or degree of high state, will start to diminish. The mother will view her daughter less than, and the daughter will start not respecting her mother in a high manner, which only opens the door for a demented thinking to start taking over. This will not be in the best interest of mother and daughter bonding. The power of doing and moving correctly together will start fading away and you do not want this to happen. This is a bad powerful force to take over.

So let's talk about how to keep the good power of a mother-daughter bond. Be the real mother that you should be. You can start by just carrying out all your responsible duties that should be done by you that require you not to expect others to be responsible for doing for you. The power of being a mother is not to complain. You just perform your given tasks every day, and the power of the daughter—she does what she knows she should do at all given matters. When the mother does matters in a correct way, the daughter does matters correctly. This motion only makes room for the power of the mother-daughter bond.

What really inspired me to write on this subject is this. I am the mother of a beautiful daughter. Every day of my life is spent being with her and sharing so many duties with her. I could only start to think about how the mother-daughter bond is one of those high, high rank positions when given the proper tools and the right guidance of right knowledge. I started understanding what it means by going to get attainment, having it which was having it every day not some days every day. It was always something I needed or something she may have needed, and what just kept sinking in my brain and her brain as well.

This mother-daughter bond is powerful—powerful all in the acceptance of us being responsible for making our own reality, only to find out this powerful bond was given us strength to keep at going and being very productive with all in operation of having faith in the unseen. Then one day, I was hit by a force like strong lightning. The Creator spoke to me: "Roshaunda, you did it. You know the power of a mother-daughter bond. Go tell the world about it."

And that is just what I did. Peace.

Mother and Daughter Awaken Intuition Relationship

I wonder—have we all heard about this magnificent, splendid, powerful word *intuition*? Webster's Dictionary defines the word *intuition* as "quick and ready, insight you can also describe as being very intuitive intuitively." Now let's tie the word *intuition* into why it is of importance when it comes to a mother-daughter relationship. Why is this awakened power of intuition so important for a mother-and-daughter relationship?

First, I will start out by saying it is a divine gift given by our Creator, the Most High, the most powerful force on earth. Intuition skills are everyday survival tools that a mother and daughter both must always operate in if they are going to do things together in fun, natural ways, as well as make things happen and, furthermore, take care of hard-core business being awakened as to how the power of intuition works. First, you can start by getting in a realm of meditation. Meditation slows your pulse rate down so you can be able to hear that still inner voice inside that's there waiting to become awakened to lead you on the direct path. I call this intuition!

A mother-daughter relationship is so much more alive when both are awakened to intuition. Sorry goes out to those who operate in a mother-daughter relationship and the powers of not being awaken in a intuition way are not present enough, or it could be that there is just no real belief in understanding and knowing this wonderful power we call intuition.

How many times have you heard others say, "I should have listened to my first instinct," or you may have said this statement yourself. The reason for saying this is most of time—or almost all the time—what that little inner voice tells us is right. From research, I found out that a high percentage of people are clueless regarding accepting its right and of how to move on quickly and keep at doing and taking care of business and completing important tasks. So why is this so important in a mother-daughter relationship? Because when this skill is developed—when a mother communicates better with her daughter, or daughters, in some cases—the answers that she may be seeking will return from her daughter quickly and swiftly, and the mother's insight will know its truth, and both will keep on moving in right action as if nothing matters, as only of what should be done and taking care of important things and deeds from mother and daughter.

This is very important because, today, we live in a world with a high percentage of distractions; everywhere and all around us, there is distraction after distraction, this or that always trying to break in or break down your focus or trip your mind up in a turbulent state of high agitation or tumult. It's one disturbance after another, and sometimes, violent acts are all around as well. We can go on in further discussion about the skills of trickery, schemes to deceive, pranks of deceptiveness, ingenious feats the mannerism the knock of duty to deceive in a cunning way to take you right off your divine path of trusting your giving true nature of intuition. For this reason, intuition is no longer a choice of not knowing and understanding how it works. That bond of mother and daughter will be snatched by many to come.

I will start by sharing what I call wolves in almighty sheep's clothing—however, in human form. These are the ones who like to approach a mother and daughter with all the wrong intentions; however, I will say and share the words that you're expecting to hear. But really, what's being practiced is the art of deception, really wanting to bring your lifestyle down to zero—to nothing in existence. When you're tapped into listening and trusting the art of intuition, you will recognize and see right off when this may be and what it is they are trying to take from you. Having the skill of developed intuition, you will spot who the takers are now. Remember, some do start off like they're going to be very pleasant and kind; however, if you allow them an inch in, they are going to take as much as they are able to get away with.

When a mother and daughter practice awakened intuition together, their unity of intuition power becomes an everyday teamwork effort. It's not going to stand for division or breakup, or that breakdown curse from others on the outside looking to see what can be taken down or brought to destruction. A mother knows that she must take time to really tune in, and her daughter is going to do the same that her mom does: tune in to her awakened-intuition self. This rhythm keeps their bond strong and good at the core of the mother-daughter bond. It's good to focus your attention inwardly to your intuitive center when others talk to you. You will be able to see if they're communicating with you or just plain downright talking at you. Nevertheless, your inner engine will recognize what's really going on and taking place, which I like to call awakened intuition.

Energy never lies. Sometimes we are the ones who lie. You just have to learn how to trust your energy and listen to it from close range. Then others will just have to take this BS somewhere else. Case in point: sometimes a lot of mothers and daughters resort to being rushers. Either the mom rushes her daughter to not be late, or the daughter is in harmony with her mother of hurrying it up, not wanting to be late. Slowing down from within will help in the area of not getting ahead of self. If you're in tune and awakened to your present reality, you can move quickly and swiftly in a smooth manner—although, at the same time, rushing is something that doesn't have to take place.

Rushing is losing control of self and your present moment. That's why when people try to rush you, it's okay to stop and tell them, "Stop trying to gain control of my present moment, my reality of having ownership, and control of my being." Let them know it's really okay that you calm yourself down. Only when the awakened intuition of your inner self is intact will a mother and daughter communicate with others from this realm of understanding, not being afraid to speak up directly and clearly when it's time. Remember, energy really is always honest. I like to say that sometimes, energy really is your friend. You just have to learn how to trust it and use it in a correct way. The more mom and daughter team up the right way, both become so in harmony to their own energy, producing the right rhythm. The result from this is right productive motion.

When a mother is awakened to her powers of intuition, she knows about the third eye chakra located between the eyebrows. Some know about the third eye; however, some don't have a clue about their third-eye chakra. Everyone has it; however, some just haven't tapped into knowing that it's real and can be put to much use in life. It's good for a mother to teach her daughter about this at a young age. When you feel and know that your daughter will understand intuition, this will teach her how to protect herself in many, many ways. When out in a public environment, awakened intuition really will help you protect yourself in many, many ways. Staying away from energy leechers will become so much of an art in itself. Why? Because there are lots of people who don't want to make an effort at discernment as to practicing passions as to what has to be gotten and how to attain it; so, therefore, energy leechers prepare to just drain who and what can be gotten away with by doing this. Energy leechers love to tear down a strong mother reality of a daughter reality of accomplishment of present now all because of recognizing that power of seeing in the now and living in the now. When a mother and daughter are really awakened to use their powers of intuition together, both having clear understanding of how the energy of intuition is used, attainment will be on an everyday rise. For both, the key ingredient is mastering trust of your own energy and staying connected to your intuition.

If you have quartz crystals, these rocks are good to carry around in your pockets or in purses or bags. These rocks carry such good energy, although you have the option to transfer your energy into your personal quartz crystal as well. Being a mom, I always had so many rocks and stones around me; so when my daughter reached the age of twelve, she owned her own quartz crystal. She would also always pick up rocks off the ground and put them in her pocket. She always had a connection with her own energy even though she was still at a young age. Now she always keeps her quartz crystal with her.

Crystals play a strong role in awakening inner intuition. It is very good for a mother and daughter to be led and guided together by their awakened intuition. Life will become a blessing after blessing for them. Others will see them as a team, which I truly believe all mothers and daughters should be—a strong team working together and helping each other manifest strong desires and dreams.

Now I am going to give you the definition of *awaken*; it means "to be awake" or "to wake up." word *awaken* means a lot in describing that genuine mother-daughter relationship in so many different situations. There are lots and lots of mother-daughter relationships that are really still in a deep, deep sleep—and we can say some of them are almost in a deep coma. This is very bad: a no-good situation. I can start by sharing constant arguments, confrontations . . . so much bad disputes with words. I know disagreement is very normal, and this type of a situation between a mother and daughter can accrue; however, when verbal and mental abuse start to set in and take place, this is, for sure, going to destroy and tear down a mother-and-daughter bond, as well as strip and take away awakened intuition.

What will happen after a long period of completing this kind of behavior is that emotional entanglements start setting in, and once the logic and reasoning starts getting demented, it only leaves room for a web of confusion, the mental breakdown of no-good understanding as to what's really going on and taking place. Just argumentation one after another at this point peace leaves their environment and welcome to the realm of mother-and-daughter bond of hell on earth. This is a bad lifestyle rhythm to make it. This is a very bad habit of a ritual of doing almost just like getting up in the morning to just brush your teeth and wash your face. You don't want to awaken to this crippled rhythm. There is no winning in this kind of motion. I am saying "stop it, don't perform this behavior."

Stay awakened to positive energy. You want to vibrate love and peace, strength—not the transformation of fatigue, fear, and stress. All that wasted energy does is put you in an early grave before you want to land there. This is why it's so important to stay focused on or in our intuitive center, feeling that natural-born high. A mother and daughter who stay awakened to intuition rejoices a lot together in spirit—a spiritual connection, a very positive energy field, an awakened power of knowing how to live in the now of happiness.

A mother and daughter must stay magnetized toward their center, doing what's really needed to keep that awakened intuition power both by being very good at following your gut and always knowing how to scope out another one's vibe verse is just going by what they're communicating; you must be real fierce about listening to that inner voice staying connected to that center point so you can feel your right life's rhythm. Synchronize and grow with that inner connection and watch how close your mother-and-daughter relationship will be positive. Staying connected to intuition is a wealthy and luxurious way of life. It is mandatory for a mother and daughter to live in a connection of harmony. This only makes and keeps their lives a joyous expression one after another. When you learn to accept and trust that you really can count on and trust the process as to how intuition really does work and how to use it for yourself, you really will benefit from this inner guidance.

A mother and daughter who use teamwork of togetherness—you really will win at living a good and happy life. This is for sure. You will bloom like a beautiful flower. You will always be sure at certain times of how you can most definitely count on your intuition as being your real friend staying deep down there in your own core soul, all the answers to what you need to know and listen to.

How many of us think we have to respond and answer so much to others? Well, guess what—we don't. Sometimes it's just okay to just let people walk away. Let them go. Being able to respond to your purpose every day is way more important; however, listening to that awakened-intuition relationship will answer so much, as well as strengthen you. This is why a mother and daughter's awakened-intuition relationship can be a guide for the sake of so many powerful moves that will only do as supposed to keeping you in a very enlightened behavior of walking in the light. A mother and daughter who are awakened to intuition really do care about one another's entrance.

A mother truly listens to her awakened intuition just to see as to what guidance every day she can keep giving her daughter to keep at following her life by. Having a real, genuine mother does make that extra step smoother. It's of greatness to help and see to it that her daughter has all the tools she may need to keep at punching in life and to get the tools needed, as well as some of the extras that life has to offer you. A daughter awakened to intuition is going to do her best to see of sense how she can help her mother win at life. The bond a daughter has for her mother is super strong; the daughter will help her mom in all business encounters, as well as how to solve personal matters. A daughter, when awakened to what's important—she's going to help her mom go after what she needs and wants very strongly in a very strong manner. Intuition gives you force and might just because you know this is what you should be moving on, and it gets to a divine point you are just so most for certain that this is the way you know to only depend on and trust. This way, your way—it becomes so clear and accurate.

Intuition awareness will stop you right down in your motion and confirm you want the best in life. You really do want to keep winning: I mean winning every day at this game we call life. Intuition tells us when a door is closed on us, or that when a door is slammed, you can easily open up the window. You will start to gain that divine confidence that's given to us most of the time by the Creator. You just start trusting it more and more: intuition power. Intuition power just keeps manifesting all the time and always.

It is so great when a mother and daughter make things happen that is of fulfillment, bringing about satisfactory performance. Awakened intuition really does open your mind to be watchful of all your great deeds and the greatness that's stored deep down in your subconscious mind. The more you tap into that intuition power—you can only come into being a great listener. The only way of gaining understanding to be able to listen well is you must pay close attention, which is why you have to watch and observe how intuition works from within your gut self. This only helps a mother and daughter gain so much extra control over that focused mind-set. What's of importance is that you give it your divine focus—all else you remove yourself from. For sure, a mother and daughter don't have any precious time to waste spinning around in foolishness, going nowhere, wasting foolish conversations with people. Don't get sucked in by wasted motion.

Always know that a mother-daughter relationship is of high meaning staying connected to how intuition work. You will gain the respect from others because others will see you are not out to use others as well as play all those wasted games that people sometimes like to play from do to not being awaken to how intuition works as well as not having knowledge of true self from within.

There's a game that some people like to play. It's called vacuum suck you into wasting your time. Stay away from this not to serve help energy it will not do you any good service at all. Sometimes in life, things can get tough and challenging; however, when a mother and daughter stay connected and awaken to using their awakened intuition force, both will gain joy in going around the mind games people like to play. Staying away from confused motion will start to be very rewarding. Knowing the use of awakened intuition shows you how to go after and chase all those dreams and ideas of your own; others waist it time is of know play and fun.

Intuition really shows you and will tell you how to steer clear away from bozo thinking. This is why awakened-intuition power is all good. This is a real good thing to have within. You will practice the art of listening for when to move out on something; performing all your important duties will be fun, and enjoying tasks as well. Yes, sometimes that one word *listen* just means so much to really benefit from it. When a mother and daughter really understand what this six-letter word really means, one of my favorite artists, Beyonce, has a beautiful song called "Listen." She sings about the word, which is a very important word. I just like to add to it. Just listen to that awakened intuition from within; you will go many, many far places. Distractions will be like rain puddles: you either walk over them or just jump right over them. Intuition tells a mother what to do. Intuition shows you and guides you how to just sometimes wait and listen. That's what listening is all about—what you need to do sometimes is just listen most of the time. Then situations start working out into right play in all areas of life, your own precious gift of life given to you by the Creator!

The Creator is the one who keeps us going and awakened to our intuition relationship. This is why a mother and daughter are supposed to practice and keep at developing intuition no matter how hard it may get for them. Just keep moving through like that tidal wave. If not, you will start to sweat the small stuff. It's there (trust me) all around us; don't even worry about it! Trust intuition and just keep on doing what you know you like to do and do best. The more you keep operating mentally from awakened intuition, you will start not to miss anything. Of all things, you will be so aware. Mother and daughter will become so in harmony together when out in the outside world because of remaining connected to inner intuition. All that you should be made aware of, you both will see.

Intuition power really does add so much more happiness into a mother and daughter's relationship. Seeking good times, enjoying and spending laughter will be a great joy. Intuition makes it all a happy pleasure of joy to really, truly help one another. Knowing and trusting that you're doing what's of best entrance is really always the smart way to go anyway. When a mom and daughter really, truly understand this, less doubt will come into action. Sometimes if a mother and daughter have not learned or grown in awakened-intuition strength, sometimes a behavior of just moving around in an emotional not-thought-out rhythm will start taking place, causing you to just do without understanding what you're doing and why you're doing it. It will start to overtake and start manifesting. This behavior is what you do not want to start in motion or practice. It only will lead to bad results. Remember, you want to get what you want and what's needed.

The power of a mother-and-daughter relationship is what you both want to win at life every day you want to receive and do things that produce a real true joy for life. And one of the first steps to this is staying awakened to your awakened intuition. There's so many divine answers to wait on to receive from within. When the inner realm of self is awakened, you will guard this center of self-knowing and understanding. Protection will be like second nature as to why it will be very important. You will be able to pick up on what a person is really speaking about. Sometimes the words people speak are really not what's being shared, so this is why you must really start to listen. Intuition teaches you how to step back, watch, and see how it is all really being played.

Awakened intuition also will teach you how to move away from what you shouldn't stay around. You will not allow others' craft of deception to deceive you because people will try to con you; however, awakened intuition points out for you to see real clearly what should be seen. You just have to stay ready to what's being viewed from almost like a 3d- vision of sight. Staying connected will keep your eyes seeing what's right in front of you, as well as to what's all around you. Having this kind of awakened personality and manner of disposition, you will start to become a distinctive, well-known person out to attain and accomplish all tasks of matter of importance.

When a mother and daughter have perspicaciousness, showing keen understanding of having discernment, watching at close-up range becomes accrued periodic growth. This helps to see and determine what to bring about as a result. Intuition-awakened strength helps you to decide or settle out whatever situation is needed. Intuition keeps you out of second-guess nature you will become so for sure at so much you will have gained that inner trust from your self to know you can, and it is okay to trust your intuition.

A mother and daughter will know what they are supposed to do on a daily basis. First, I can start by sharing knowing how to get along with each other and, most importantly, knowing how to communicate with each other using the power of mother-and-daughter language—the methods of combining information for clear communication. When a mother and daughter are awakened for having and understanding power of choice of words, making their reality becomes a run at life, a go for it just because their courage will be just that: to make sure of being able to take action and step forward. Getting it done moving forward will be automatic progress, upward mobility for mother and daughter calling it out loud, doing what should be done from the both of them recognizing strength from rhythm of lack of strength. The power of intuition will only build good, strong, firm character having the authority to call it out as you see it just seeing what's needed for what it is and staying at doing what you should be doing and not taking individuals' fake paper play-play hat for more than nothing, because if you do, your moves in life will become crippled by other fake insults of attack.

Doing daily chores and activities throughout the day will consist of you being very awakened in using your intuition skills. There has always been this quote that "a woman's work is never done," or I like to say "a daughter's work is never finished," as most of the time, a mother has something for her daughter to do and complete as well. Being and staying awakened to the power of intuition will gain you so much respect just because others can see and will tell that you are awakened. Some will know that it's intuition strength, and some will just be shocked to see someone look or stare them straight back into their eyes.

When a mother and daughter are both awakened, it builds a daughter to have good character and self-esteem when her mother looks her straight in the eyes when they are communicating. It is very much of importance for a mother and daughter to represent respect when out doing daily business transactions. It's good to be taken seriously. One reason for this is so that life can be very subdued. In life, most of the time, you really will be judged from how your appearance and manners are. It's a fact that people will judge you whether you want them to or not—however, sometimes it's possible not to be happy about it. However, it's just how it can be. So therefore, staying awakened to intuition will only help you be and become more accurate. Being free from error, this only makes a mother's and daughter's lives a lot more easy at times.

Life can be fun; however, it can really be very tough as well. Sometimes we must really punch back hard to get and really have attainment, and being awakened does open lots of doors for a mother and daughter to walk in and attain when a mother and daughter make daily effort as to what life really is about. Doing all those things of importance helps them refrain from that force of long, drawn-out, go-nowhere gossip. I mean, of course, a mother and daughter have small talk and joke around about what is shown to them on an everyday basis; however, living in gossip and drowning in it is of no good behavior for a mother and daughter to operate in. It's almost like suffocating in an ocean of water.

Being awakened to intuition power will help you really see just how gossip motion is itself a very weak force; however, if you're given over to that force of gossip, then it's an energy that will overpower you if you stay away from it, or at least make conscious effort to not practice it. You will have control to stand up and not fall down in it with others, just because of them wanting company from it. A mother and daughter both have strength and authority to not be crippled and weakened down by BS gossip. Go toward what you like and stay away and refrain from what you don't like. The more awakened you are, you will have the strength to take care of your own business—not someone else's. Staying a lot in nature, walking around in nature a lot also helps you from refraining from gossip as well. It helps you keep your own mind clear so you learn how to be responsible for your own inner gossip inside yourself that must be kept in mental check. Your own inner self is enough of a difficult task to take on; this is hard—understanding all and most of the time anyway. A mother really does teach her daughter how to stay, as of remaining in her own lane in life, not worrying and taking in not necessary of not worrying and taking in unnecessary of no worthy conversation that's not important no weak water down inner communication. You must stay connected too your intuition this will keep you on your guarded post in life.

Staying connected toward your own self is very important. When a mother stays in her own lane as well, her daughter will only grow and bloom more to gain and really respect her mother. A mother in her lane of taking care of her own business will keep taking the time to make sure she does all that's needed. She will take the time to teach her daughter how to bake a cake, and sometimes, she will even bake a cake for her daughter. Just to show her how special she really is.

A lot of times when I go outside and I hear all the gossip at local supermarkets and stores like Target—when you hear that gossip of women sharing how much of not having time to accomplish different tasks—most of the time, it's because of not remaining in their own lane as to what should be of their stretching every day at getting things done. Don't let others use up your energy. If you don't use your energy, others will.

When I view how energy really works, you only get so much per day anyway—so why not use it in a good way, and in a fun and exciting way? Don't keep your emotions down and out in a puddle of others' muddiness and mental confusion. You will become awakened to all that's around you, and of just how much time a mother and daughter have to take care of important business, as well as fun of excitement. Remember, on earth you get one life. Why waste precious time when you can be spending so much time enjoying, listening to your awakened intuition? That's why it's just so darn important for a mother and daughter to be awakened to inner intuition. This will keep them both at always practicing at having a good, meaningful relationship. You must understand how separation really works, knowing the difference between what should be done and what should not be done. Staying awakened to intuition shows you what to do and what not to waste your time doing. When you don't listen to your intuition, others will have you controlled by their inner dark world of madness.

Take a stand, mother and daughter. Live life. Enjoy your lives. Do positive things. Act on good emotions. Keep performing good tasks in the world. Travel together. Help each other paint your rooms the color you always wanted your room to be. Enjoy that cup of coffee because—remember—the world is here for us to enjoy and partake in it. Just always know that having a connection with intuition will keep you safe and protected in many ways, just because it is the power of divine inner listening!

The Closeness between
Mother and Daughter

There's a wise old saying about the power of being close with someone. You know, I have watched so many people in the world today who are very close with their pets. I see so many people walking their dogs on an everyday routine with the connection of closeness. We live in a big and beautiful world where we are surrounded, enclosed all around by the realms of beautiful nature, the closeness of trees and flowers—nature everywhere. However, how often do we see 3-D close-ups in doing daily living? Will we come in contact with seeing the closeness between a mother and daughter!

Some of my readers may say yes, this connection is viewed all the time. From my journey of doing research, I see this real closeness at a very small percentage. Of course, there are lots of individuals who operate under labels, titles, words—there are just so many of them. We can start with the word *mother*. When some of us think of the word *mother*, we can say it means more of, or the essence of, how a mother produces and brings about. Now I will agree with this statement for being very true; however, let's take the word *mother* much further and define it by *Webster's Dictionary.*

Mother: "a female parent source that gives birth to cherish or protect." The first degree of respect you are due and owed is because of you giving birth. Much respect is highly due to all women just for performing this high and esteemed state that alone makes women so tough, beautiful, and bold. Okay, good—you did it! However, guess what? Now that you did it don't stop there. That same pain spent giving birth is your welcome into the world of being a real and true mother. Pain in life will not stop. Being a mother always requires birth acts of faith and acts of you being brave—which is why your second birth is that you must now, for the rest of your entire life, keep developing that closeness with your daughter, which is the same automatic closeness you experience when you hold your baby for the first time.

Some may say "Oh, that's not hard to do. This is an easy task." However, guess what? So many slip back out from that bond of closeness and don't even realize it, not seeing at all how far they have fallen away from that divine closeness between a mother and daughter. It is very sad, but this motion has become the very proof of evidence, clearly obvious if you're watching, paying close attention at what is viewed in the world today.

A mother has to always do her best at making effort in the area of making sure she keeps closeness with her daughter. The minute—the second—a mother is done delivering the war, the battle begins. You must be very determined at establishing that closeness. It may not appear to be a different task because the baby is new. This is your newly born special baby—your own child, not your friend's. It can appear easy at first; however, as you keep going further into this duty of constant motion, time shows you how much work is really going to have to take place. Lots of joy, lots of great rewards—however, there is still a lot of strong work involved in it.

At the stage of the baby crying and crying, and you sometimes have to keep waking up from your sleep to attend to your baby . . . Please don't get mad. This is really just a beginning stage of preparing you for all the work you are looking at viewing further down the path of the closeness you will keep developing within your mother-daughter connection. A lot of times, when a new baby arrives home, so many people want to hold the baby and get extra close; but nevertheless, if you're not the mother, it is not always such a good idea. The only real closeness should be between the mother and baby. The mother has to make sure she is allowing her protective energy around her child. The closeness has to keep merging. This good behavior that a mother and daughter may practice at their beginning stage is only what will keep their closeness to continue in the right way. If not, trust me, wolves in sheep's clothing will come in and take that bond of closeness down that a mother and daughter have and share. Some will do just that and not care at all—not care 1 percent. This is just how it is with some people in the world today! This is why a mother must never give up on her daughter and stop caring, no matter what situations are taking place.

A daughter, most of the time, will always need something from her mother. It's just a proven fact. So, mothers, keep that divine closeness with your daughter. Laugh at those out there in the world who want you to think it's not important to have that closeness, when you know how important and special that closeness is outside wrong insecure forces will not be able to get in and tear, destroy, or knock you down. You will have developed a backswing at breakdown motion. Every day a mother and daughter have to practice the art of closeness in a civilized manner, a mother will make sure that her daughter has the tools she needs in order to accomplish daily or occurring tasks, making sure things are done and complete, staying away from deception and not allowing the deceiving and deceptive humans the control over giving divine life from the Creator.

The righteous conduct and behavior a daughter brings to her mother is respect and obedience, willing to do what's right that is asked from her by her mother. When a daughter has that closeness with her mother, she will follow the commands and guidance in accordance with right and proper behavior, which is so important. Doing right and moving in right motion will produce a heavenly behavior; doing wrong will produce a satanic rhythm, a motion of darkness, which only blocks a mother and daughter from being able to see clearly together. It is a proven fact that if Satan's force gets in, it can cause a mother and daughter to be pulled from their closeness. Darkness will overtake their bond, and Satan's force of evil will come right in and let the games of confusion begin.

When a mother and daughter start losing their close connection, evil will do all that it can to get in and start destroying and start tearing down slowly. However before you know it now it is destruction that gets in between the mother and daughter. This is a not a good way of conduct for a mother and daughter to operate in, nothing of meaning and will and of high important purpose will be able to get done their relationship will be based around trap after trap all due to not keeping Satan's evil force out. So, therefore, others' wicked energies will be transferred to the mother and daughter, and the closeness of the bond of a mother and daughter will be gone totally, of no good use at all. What you will see and hear is a high level of argumentation. Every minute, every second, this will start to be based around high inclined confrontation, not knowing how to handle situations in a right, civilized manner.

Closeness really will keep wrong out, I always tell my daughter. Just because Satan calls you up does not mean you have to answer. Stay on your right path so you can keep getting your rewards that living a good, right life has to offer you. When a mother and daughter do have that closeness, the power of listening is so in harmony with their motion. A mother and daughter have to take care of business. They must get things done and move out and around instructed motion—motion that's not structured will not be able to break down right rhythm. Keep your eyes on looking close range at the bond of closeness that has manifested. The baits that haters will use to try to get in and next to you will not work. You will see so straight and right clear through them all. Wasted energy of madness will have to be taken and dumped somewhere else; however, not on that closeness of right between a mother and daughter.

So much power in the art of closeness—when practiced the right way of doing something anything right—will always expose what's not right. When a mother and daughter have a real and authentic genuine closeness, it will develop into both of them walking in the aura of confidence. The mother and daughter will not need self-assurance from anyone. When you need to depend on getting self-assurance from others out in the world, that's not a good behavior to practice and walk in. Others will pick up on you being codependent for looking for that rhythm from someone else, and what's going to happen is it will allow others to open up that door of deception and manipulation.

When someone thinks that you can really be conned, a person will try to gain the title of influence over you. You don't have to allow and accept this kind of low self-esteem and worthless conduct. This is why a real mom teaches her daughter how to have control over herself, and a mother knows that she must always keep at practicing the art of self-maintenance, self-control. Losing control is not the way you want to travel. You want to always maintain that self-control, and one key ingredient for having strong substances in this area is having self-knowledge. Knowing yourself and understanding who you are will give you real assurance and lots of confidence.

When a mother and daughter have that divine closeness, the mother is the guide for her daughter's behavior. With that being said, she is responsible for management behavior in their relationship. Having strong knowing of how her daughter is, she is much able to help in directing her daughter on the path of getting things done and taking care of business in right conduct and right manner, and the daughter really does trust her mother because she knows her mother has real concern. She can see clearly that her mother takes delight in helping her daughter succeed in all areas of accomplishment and achievement.

A certain percentage of young teenage girls will go out into the world and look for a relationship to get in with the opposite gender, only to find out that they're walking into a dysfunctional relationship, wanting closeness so bad and so extra intense. However, in some cases, she will go into the so-called relationship blind. She will sometimes even end up getting pregnant, only to find out that she still does not receive that closeness she wants so badly from the young male. Most of the time, she will still find herself being very unhappy and not being able to reach any fulfillment at all, still never really being truly satisfied. All because deep from within, there should first have been a real bond of closeness between the mother and daughter in the first place.

Anyway, from doing careful research, most males like to bond with the female gender from the waist down anyway, and will go off on a girl if she demands bonding from his heart. A male—most of the time—is extra, extra slow like a snail or how a turtle moves. Seriously, they are not in any rush at all about bonding from the heart; so this is why that real closeness between the mother and daughter is of so much importance. For example, if the young daughter decides that she must get pregnant in order to get this bond of closeness from this young male, it's really not going to happen most of the time. So what happens sometimes is the young girl will abort the child if she thinks it's no use for a connection with the male, or in some cases, she will carry the child full term and discover that even though she has had the child, the bonding is still not right with the young male. She has the child now. What only happens to her is she goes about being and feeling real disturbed from within, only to find out that she still is not happy because of not still experiencing real happiness—that closeness she so deep down in her own soul wants so bad, although feeling as though she does deserve it.

I am not saying that now that the young girl has a newborn baby, she can't come into real bonding and continue to grow and bond the right way with her newborn baby. However, a very strong percentage don't do this. Some still just blame themselves and the baby as to why things are not working out and going the right way, all due to what really takes place and starts at zero before you can get to number 1. That close bond between the mother and daughter really has to be the proper and correct way. That's why I am writing this book as of now, because deep down, I speak these words from the realm of truth. So I know these are true facts and need to be dealt with, and someone really has to speak on these, and Ms. Roshaunda has been called out to do so by the Creator.

You know, a lot of times as I take long walks, or sometimes I may take a ride on the train—I am going to be as honest as possible about this serious matter. A lot of young girls—I will say starting somewhere from age thirteen on up—I am going to speak about what I see, what I view most of the time. I do not see enough mothers out around as vanguards or chaperones in large social environments. It's more important than one really would think, for the daughter to be around her mother more sometimes in public. I believe it is still a mother's duty to always, as much as possible, peek in on her daughter's lifestyle. You need to be present in your daughter's daily walk, sometimes just to see where you must help her more in becoming a better person in society just so she can keep winning at this game called real life.

Sometimes in order to do things right get to the top at the highest level, you need someone around you that's really real and does really care—otherwise, it's just so easy to become bombarded by what's fake, and this only blocks you from continuing at going further. It will become very difficult at reaching high maximum standard!

I am just going to straight-out say it. Most other young girls really don't know what real friendship is, and most other young girls without strong guidance and protection and right structure are really all about competition. Competition without right structure is really just straight out about doing whomever is around them in! In a way of not really caring and soul heartly straight about themselves. It's really not about maintaining, or having, friendships. It's about me getting what I want first, and if I have to, I will knock you down, keep you down, and while I attain—or if I start attaining more—I will stop calling or communicating with you in a real blunt way. This is just how it is. This was never real friendship anyway. It was all about draining someone, and you allowed me to do just that; and that's what I did. Just because you allowed it to happen.

Another common situation I have viewed and watched most of the time was when young girls—some time when they're around the age of sixteen through and around twenty—the so-called friendship ends and is completely over and goes straight downhill when a male shows up on the scene. The competition between both girls go up for real, and both really do lose serious control. Back to what I mention, it wasn't friendship. From the beginning, it was competition. I am not saying young girls shouldn't know each other, or even do some events together, but nevertheless, I am first saying learn to be very watchful and observant for yourself. So you can keep moving on in your day-to-day lifestyle and not get caught up in others sewing buttons over your eyes so you can't see and make out who is truly good for yourself.

Moms, make a better effort at keeping the closeness between your daughters' relationships. Help keep your daughters from falling down when all you have to do is keep showing or demonstrating how you walk right and straight up and conduct yourself properly. As I write now, I really enjoy thinking about young gymnast Gabrielle Douglas. At sixteen, she did a major world accomplishment. Like I mentioned before, Gabrielle Douglas was very present, very aware, living in the now with strong right guidance and a strong connection that kept her and her mother close, even though close but not entanglement of wrong motion and behavior. Her mother really did allow her daughter to be and become what she really is good at. Competition with other young girls was done the right way: all of them competing for something they loved doing. However, they were not trying to trip one another down and making no effort at seeing how to get back up.

Why wasn't this the case? Structure was around them in the proper manner, with right adult supervision. You may compete however you wish them good luck and move forward to your next level of lifestyle. You don't get stuck and stop and start draining others, which is not a good product or right behavior. I am sharing this because that closeness between a mother and daughter can honestly prevent the mother and daughter from wasting precious time, because a real mother doesn't talk about unnecessary subjects and perform wasted acts. Not important duties and tasks.

A real mother doesn't lose her substance of energy carelessly. She knows it is not about being of no further use of waste. A real mother is always making strong efforts to better herself because she knows if she is always seeking to empower herself, she will be better able to really help her daughter and remain and keep their mother-and-daughter relationship close. Thinking for a moment about Gabrielle Douglas, the world's great gymnast, I am quite sure most of my readers may have heard that there was a high percentage of those naysayers. I'd like to give the names of who were really talking about how Gabrielle Douglas's hair looked bad and messed up. I really could not believe what was being said about her; it just didn't really make any common sense. How could such foolish conversations take such place at the same time all the great, positive hard work she had swung up and done? At the same time, this beautiful young girl had already reached her highest performance of excellence at her pinnacle, the highest point of winning in the game called life; and all that could be said by those who really suffered from negative energy was talk about her hair! How sad and how disturbing; this thinking pattern could have been such a strong leak out in the world.

This is my example of confused motion and energy when it's not directed and aimed in the right proper direction, a behavior that so many young girls and some women gender operate in when the right way and right correction of motion and energy is not made manifest to them. Some young girls are just not taught right and proper conduct from day 1, the early part of their years—so, therefore, their mothers, most of the time, are lost in many ways as to how to show and give their daughter, or daughters, the instruction manual as to how to live a good life as well as practice at moving according to right productivity of action. This is why it is so important for a mother and daughter to have the right proper closeness in righteous motion and righteousness of conduct.

From my doing so much research being out in the field on the streets, what I am starting to really notice is that the female gender is of preying on each other a lot, of using and abusing, taking from each other, a lot of backstabbing coming from other young girls as well as a confused class of older women who, in some way, still operate in a childlike thinking most of the time. I observe, watch, and see it from a clear point of view, preying on each other, or behaving as female predators taking advantage of one's coming into certain development, areas that can take some time. However, females are doing their best to snatch other females' rites of passage.

Myself growing up in my younger years, I was a majorette: a baton twirler. We did not snatch each other's baton or, a better way to put it, take someone else's baton. You would throw it to them or pass it. There is a process of passing. You have to be given a right to have a pass or another right way to speak on it, given proper permission of entry to have the right to enter or come in. You don't just welcome yourself if there was not given to you an invite or an invitation. Without the invitation, you don't get a pass in the door. This is just right manners that have to be taught by a mother and passed straight down to her daughter or, in some cases, her daughters.

In my younger years, no one would dare just come up to me and just snatch or take my baton from me. You would get your own baton, and your right was to protect it because it was yours. Today, I see so much of young girls and mothers snatching and taking that crown of rites of passage—your divine birthright—as to how, what, when, and where do I go and how to get to the next levels of living, not wanting to share right information or just plain right very down low as to not helping the mind-set is get it on your own, or if your not going to stay around and allow the manipulation game willing to be played on you, then get on, all in the name of friendship.

This is not friendship. This is why a lot of times, others will get so seriously mad when manipulation can't be played on you. Stand up for yourself. You don't have to fall down in an ethically wrong code of living—you don't have to and must not do this. If others want you to, if you think it's just not right, don't bite no one else's bullet. And this is real: true teaching a mother will teach her daughter. When that closeness between a mother and daughter is glued in right thinking, right conduct, and right behavior, both the mother and daughter are more easy discerned about keeping wrong out and not letting it in to have play in and around their lives. There is no time, no room for the crab, crab, crab pulling-down mind-set. It's just not going to be taking place, but the art of business will be taken care of, the real game played in life.

When a mother and daughter appreciate the art of how a business transaction really does reward their motion of righteousness and productivity, their value of being grateful for having a positive closeness for being mother and daughter does really increase. Both will sit stronger down in value of what appreciation is really, truly all about! I do believe that the reason for why there are so many dysfunctional relationships in our world today is due to a basic and fundamental lack of having normal common sense. When a mother and daughter have sound mental capacity, automatic detection of when something is not right and correct will manifest immediately. The mother and daughter both will know how to direct and move it away and keep that motion from entering the atmosphere of right. Their mother-and-daughter bond will have an aura of protection around it that being able to move forward in the world and build other happy, right relationships with others in a positive and right connection.

As I view different kinds of relationships that different types of people are in, some are happy and good for the soul, while others looked like a liquor drain every day of their lives. Now you may be asking yourself, what does she mean when she shares liquor drain? I will explain it to you right now as good and as clear as possible. Some people have no discernment skills at all, or they just don't use their discernment skills to see the actual benefits of self. Therefore, having no control over allowing liquor-drainer individuals in their lives—so what happens is when you are in this kind of low-energy relationship with someone, rather it's a mother-and-daughter drain relationship, husband-wife relationship, or so-called best-friend relationship, you always feel drained when you walk away from that person. The longer you are around them, your energy becomes really zapped, and before you realize it, you have no energy for yourself to take care of all your different tasks of matters that are of real importance to you and good for you.

Liqoud drainers, these type of individuals don't care about draining you and will do just what I mentioned to you if you don't stand up in the beginning will make it a divine effort to take from you in all kinds of ways, being able to get away with doing just so. Some of them will act and impose as if they really want to know you or have a good relationship with you; however, deep down in their soul knowing of that this is just a down right down to cover up don't fall for it. Liqoud drainers don't care about others the way a person with a good heart and of good character does, which is why knowing yourself is very much of importance once you pick up on mental drainers and energy drainers. You will learn how to keep them far out. Otherwise, their willingness and delight of destroying putting an end to you being in positive high thinking will seriously dimension. This is like being at the playground for them, or riding their favorite ride at Six Flags Magic Mountain sounds a little off balance; however, this is so much of truth, and what happens at most is when you stand up to these energy drainers, you will see there was really not too much of like for you anyway. It is just their way of saying "Thank you for letting me drain you. You know the deal, I am on to the next soul I will take delight in draining."

I have said all this for one main reason why. The importance of closeness for mother and daughter is so important because of strong recognition—the act of recognizing the state of being a person is in at all times. You really will be able to take notice and see who that person really is and most certainly know what their hidden agenda really is in my conclusion. Wake up, mother and daughter. Work as a strong team. Keep that closeness pure and right. Keep your divine bond in use of right, and no one will be able to steal and take your closeness down. You will have the strength and power to make Satan do a dangerous U-turn. Always remind yourself of how the closeness between a mother and daughter is divine and divinely given.

What Makes a Mother
and Daughter Special

We have all heard that word before—*special*—or been told by someone throughout our lives how special we may be. See and take a view at what this word really means.

Special: "unusual or unique, particularly favored, set aside for a particular use." Explaining the word *special*, I guess I would have to share just being different, not the same! For this reason explains in clear detail why a mother-and-daughter relationship is really so special. There is no other relationship out in the world that's of your relationship that you're in—that's of pure a state as the mother-and-daughter relationship. Which is why you guard it, you protect it, and you make it grow. You work at it to produce positive results and wanted positive actions of all good kinds to make present of manifestation. Reason being highly favored is a fraction of explaining just how unique this bond of mother and daughter really is, which is why you watch out for those who want, or will try, to get around you in a corrupt bribe debased way. Remember always when something is special good of its own kind some see, or view what's of difference as something just to mess with to see if it can be tore down brought down break down or to splint in half really to all extreme destroy!

Having special ability, you must accept it, claim it, and most of all, you must certainly know you have it and stay connected to its presence of it so you can always be on the lookout for what's special and what's a gift from the Creator—titled special connection given from above, the Most High. When a mother and daughter know the depth of not wasting precious time, both will greatly cherish all the different tasks that must be performed by them. Every moment, every second, will be of much value when you do performance, carrying out right deeds and action. Valuing your time will be like second nature; the results of your action will manifest the way you want them to. Mother and daughter will have no time to worry over small stuff, staying ascertained and very determined about accomplishing short-time goals.

Long-time goals will be what's of most important for a mother and daughter. Chasing special tasks will be a strong motivator to make it happen, as well as living in the happening, staying in the knowing, and watching close range at all positive progress. Having this special mother-and-daughter connection can be of so much fun, even though there are a lot of important responsibilities and tasks that have to be performed from most of your golden time. However, having laughter and lots of fun will make proof to show just how special a mother and daughter really are. You can come together to go watch musical plays live with orchestra the Shen Yun is a very beautiful, astonishing, incredibly striking play for a mother and daughter to go see together. It is a very elegant show with so much fun involved; you really will enjoy it.

Mothers, you should always show and demonstrate special behavior for your daughter or daughters. Actions sometimes speak loud volumes when someone does and goes in action with you more than on just speaking at you—action deeds do stretch further than communication. Sometimes communication is good; however, bold action is very important. I love to hear President Obama share that it's time for some action. He says it so in harmony with my self-nature, because he knows action is bold self-assertiveness. A statement of self how much your in action or the action you take, you really prove and back them up with words you may speak on most of the time. An action statement does prove how much you really care.

I was once told love is what it does, not what it says. The word *love* is a beautiful word; however, when love is expressed, it is of a much more powerful force. Most who have received this expression can really relate to what I just shared. This is what makes a mother and daughter so genuine in their relationship being of a special breed just because of its right, natural closeness. Arguments and never-ending negative confrontations should not be the real center core of a mother-daughter relationship. Positive motion and right, good conduct and a behavior of much-earned respect are the core—all else is of bad conduct, which only will just produce negative standards. The more you accept that you have a special bond, you will just keep doing special work and special tasks. Remember there will be the kind of people I like to call bloodthirsty, seeking leeches, who appear as when you are communicating with them that their conversation is meaningful and that they really have your interest at heart. However, they're really behaving like freshwater worms that feed on blood. So in this case, there is a motion of your energy getting drained on as if you owe your life force to them.

Be very aware, when you have this mother-and-daughter special bond, be careful and be cautious as much as possible. Watch out for the leeches. Trust me—they're out there, and they're hoping you don't know what you have is really divine and a special reason for their wanting to come right in and suck your energy dry. Remember there is no need and room for this kind of nonsensical mental behavior. If you see and feel this act of downward lower place of draining motion, move on and keep it stepping; and whatever you do, do not let these types of individuals in any further, because if you do, there's going to be some serious problems that will cause all kinds of negative confrontations. Humans who have that leech mentality love to express a lying conversation and transfer it on to you so you can g into an argument with them just to take you out of good chara and come down as low as where they're at. Keep the leeches out allow a leech to feed off good energy. If you do, you're the on going to walk away drained, and it's just not really worth

In no way do people with leech mentalities want yo and realize how special that mother-and-daughter bo makes it special. Becoming aware through know your senses will show you what is and what yo and accept when you start claiming that special life. You will have strength and courage to take on special tasks. Remember, in life, yo for setting the kind of stage you want. the ones who set your stage in your l and sometimes be very determined t orchestrate and arrange your life for what they may see best for it. You have special rights of just claim to respectfully decline what others say should go!

There are special codes for a mother and daughter to have standards around their lifestyle of how their living arrangement is performed and being performed. Knowing how to sit in right structure is very important, and knowing how to put a stop or to end another from trying to pull you out of your structure only for their benefit to feel accomplished, as if being able to exercise bend breakdown motion over you know that you're in their presence when you master sitting in your own structure. You can so feel if someone is trying to pull you to perform this act of weakness, which is why you will not allow others to have governance, or rule over your essence in a sovereign, supreme way, knowing this information is what will keep your mother-and-daughter bond special because of having the right information and knowing what's making an effort at pulling from your own reality the power of feeling guilty will not have access in a way of making you feel feelings of guilt. You will have become so guilt-free. You will just keep on moving upward in special motion ᵒur own control and ownership of your life, which only opens ᶠᵒʳ rewardship of doing and having a lot of special time ᵉʳ and daughter, discussing special topics, taking ᵗᵒᵍᵉᵗʰᵉʳ together, discussing with each other ᵃlways seek and pursue higher

ˢᶦtuations they're
ᵒund them
of entrance
invite, or an
hat to do and
ᴐnfirmation of
ᵍether, working
enjoying all that
ᴐf making things
s of different ways!
᠎ daughter go watch
ter. So much joy and
᠎ll as after the showing

ᵉᵗ
ᶜter
, don't
ᵉ who is
ᵗ.
ᵈ to perceive
ᵈ is, and what
ᶦⁿg how to use
should recognize
reward around your
do special deeds and
ᵘ are the one responsible
ᵉ, although others are not
Remember others may try
ᵉ power over your life, to
ʰave power over your life, to

of the movie, going home and having an intelligent showing of discussion of one's point of view. A very good thing to do for a mother and daughter is just always at practice of keeping their intellectual power of knowing and thinking in right harmony. One of the main reasons why a mother-and-daughter relationship is so special is the art of keeping their emotions in check together just so and being able to raise their minds up together so they're able to do things right and think given situations through in good understanding, to have and maintain better action of moving through and having a clear action plan of method for accomplishment of moving in the realm of now!

I have been around and observed so many different mother-daughter relationships of action of right-now motion, and it is just a crying shame that they do not know that their relationship of mother-and-daughter connection should be special. This is not the case. High argument is always taking place over louding each other goes on constant their conversation is just of no use most of time not discussing what's of important to make things better at every moment every second of their life better for each the mother and daughter and sometimes for daughters. It's just so downright sad to witness this behavior because, most of the time, an onlooker sees this kind of commotion. Those who are operating in this twisted trip-up, confused emotions are really given out strong, dangerous, hard looks of not wanting nothing to be told to them very sad, why is this so sad, because this is a behavior practice of wrong that is of operation so long until now their thinking is of it's okay to behave in this motion and talk of accordance I am here now, right now in presence of words writing this information to inform it's wrong, not right, and it's a big rob of steal that it's just simply wrong and not right.

A lot of wasted energy and time is lost and cannot be gotten back. Every minute and every second is of precious time and cannot be gotten back. Eternity is in every minute or every second. I like to think it is, anyway. The life that a mother and daughter choose to live is very special. A mom and daughter can both purchase a house right next door to each other and work in unity together, sit down and drink tea and coffee together, and at the same time, be of no distraction and no disturbance. The daughter will have total control over her own life, and her mother will keep at becoming more of who she is and sit at time to pass down that unique, genuine wisdom and knowledge to her daughter in a much respectful way that she will still have space away from her mother, although still close of sharing that special mom-daughter bond. Some people understand it, and some don't, just because their perception of this idea is not clear. So there are those who remain in the dark mental realm of thinking.

A mother who resides next door to her daughter, or who lives in a house down the street from her daughter, will only make this an everyday ritual to not get in each other's business there will be respect for each other's new lives and living space disrespectful behavior will not take place when a mother and daughter respect their bond. A bond of right conduct is totally different from thinking from that perspective of being codependent. This way of behavior only blocks motion and disturbs motion, all of action of right versus wrong. My dad's mother lived next door to her mom, and their relationship wasn't codependent—both were close, however, not codependent. I remember walking off the steps from my dad's sister's porch right on to my grandmother's house right next door. I thought this was so cool, and as of being an adult right now, it is cool for a mother and daughter to live near nothing like having a strong support system you can count on—because it has your back and is just there for you when the going gets tough, which it does sometimes.

I just like to call it old-fashioned life. It stares us right back in the face every single day and where free with either what do I do now, or what move do I make to keep on moving further. This reason explains why a mother-and-daughter relationship is absolutely of very much importance. A real mom always has those special-recipe instructions for helping her daughter prepare a delicious, very pleasing taste of an aromatic meal. It's always a delight to be near great-tasting food at such close range. And sometimes the daughter will return that reward to her mom as well, knocking at her mom's door and announcing, "I baked your favorite cake for your birthday. Come over for a celebration." So there are just so many reasons and ways to do things to keep that mother-and-daughter relationship special.

The more you live together in the now in a pleasant rhythm of motion, the better; and more rewards will keep manifesting in and around your lives. You will go on fun vacations together, take lots of beautiful cruises together, and enjoy lots of fun and laughter together when a mother and daughter reach a high level of civilization. There are just so many fun rewards both will do and enjoy. Doing it will almost become like second nature—to look out for each other. Helping out will just be a normal task of fun. I tell you, this is the right way a mother and daughter will want to live.

You must keep at having a strong, developed radar at seeing who you're around and what's trying to show up and what was to be and around your developed structure. If not, it will welcome itself right in and start seriously draining you at a high rate and in a real extreme manner. This is knowing your self-worth is of so much importance because you will not be much afraid to govern and live your life at how you choose to live it. You will know it's very much okay to get up and regulate your beautiful life the way you want it to go and proceed throughout your choice of activities every day.

It's not illegal yet to think. We all are entitled to freedom of choice, so why not choose and plan our days out the way we want to see results? Yes, proper and right behavior, as I just mentioned, is absolutely of good deeds for a mother and daughter to operate in this kind of thinking every day to produce a happy environment. It's so important for a mother and daughter to know how to make the right, proper moves in a fast way, and they must be very active and on point when doing so—very sharp and very on cue, very keen and very much knowing when it's time to move on. Moving in action in a motion of harmony only helps a mother and daughter do battle the right way when out in the world, making things happen in a good, productive way.

A mother and daughter have real good, special radars as to what both should be doing at all times. Remember there is a good force field, and of course, we all know who that adversary is, that bad force opposing and in opposition to whatever it is a mother and daughter does their best to make right and do right. This is why it's so important for mother and daughter to be ready and prepared to box, put on their boxing gloves and go for what is known as what's right for winning in this real game called life that we all must face and wake up to every day! That's why teatime has always been of so much importance for a mother and daughter to make time for and spend every hour and every second of enjoying this magic moment of their time being spent together. This teatime is what I sometimes like to call their golden bonding time that does really mean so much to both, because taking the time to come together to make all things happen for the good and, most certainly, for sorting out and getting rid of and keeping all others BS and drama out of their beautiful lives. I hope understanding of what's been said and spoken in words of written expression is clear.

Another way of special bonding for mother and daughter is taking a long train ride and talking together in light conversation and, at the same time, expressing what's of view to looking throughout the train window. This exercise is of good service because this view out the train window is of the power of now—paying attention and watching as to what's taking place and what's really going on right now! A train ride has always held a position of being able to do something special that produces results of fun. It keeps you connected to your slow-paced rhythm pulse as the train moves fast. A good, long train ride is just a perfect thing for a mother and daughter to most definitely do together—a good and fun way to stare back at the world. However, at the same time, you should not let the world pass you by as if it doesn't exist. It's such a rewarding task and experience to partake in life in positive ways and participate in positive, good events and journey in life. It's all fun and good enjoyment and wise and good use of time. A mother knows the importance of valuing time. A daughter knows how special that time factor is as well because her mother made sure she came into understanding that value at such a young age of knowing and doing what you should do. As I like to say—something meeting the mark!

We all have heard that statement over and over that divine apples don't fall too far from the tree, unless it's on that hill. So what I am sharing most of the time is a daughter is really so much like her mother anyway, so why shouldn't mothers do their very best at being the best of a good example a mother can be for her daughter—or, in some cases, daughters as well. A mother will always hold a special, unique gift of title. So do your absolute, definite best job at enjoying being the best mom as possible, expressing and absorbing all high-quality rewards of it, so much joy and fun as well when of sometime if just a guide is given of reward and excitement of performing this task can help you out in so many tremendous ways, so this is why I myself, Queen Roshaunda, am writing and expressing these words because of all and so much concern.

I do truly have concern for the mother-daughter relationship. It is now, and will always be, very important and one of my concerns. Which is why I write and bring this information to the world. As women, we are the responsible parties for showing and demonstrating our worldwide concern for having strong care for mothers and daughters all over the world. I do believe when a woman does think in high order and is given over to high standards, there is so much of high credit that will be given to her. It all starts with women just simply making a strong, real stance of what is truly their belief system! Living by a set of rules that are good in such a way whereas these rules help them and also show manifestation that their rules are of much benefit to them for their lives.

When a mother knows how important it is for her to go all out of her way to make sure her daughter has the right tools she needs as well as to making sure her daughter keeps observing what's going on and taking place in her life, there will be just so many, many rewards her daughter will bring back to her mother to show her so much of how much she really is so appreciative of all the hard work and sacrifice that she viewed done by her mother.

A good daughter never takes her mom for granted. She is always doing her best to show how much care she has for her mother. This is only but one of the attributes of what makes a mother-and-daughter relationship a one-of-a-kind, special, unique fabric. A mother-and-daughter relationship is woven together in a bond of trust and respect and, in reality together, really making it most certainly work in a demonstration of showing the world. There is a lot of seriously committed teamwork effort at a one-on-one level of doing. A dedication as to what really will be done and what must be done. When it's all said and done, the real outcome between a mother and daughter, you really do want to have each other's back through all times and all around every given situation that life brings to you at face value.

A daughter is going to produce so much greatness when she knows her mother is really counting on her and being that motivated cheerleader cheering her daughter on that "you can do it." I mean voicing it will give it all you've got. You can really accomplish and attain what it is you need, as well as all those fun things of desire. This kind of support can only but produce a happy daughter.

A mother gives and takes glory in knowing that her daughter is obedient to truth and of having clear judgment of who her mother is. This keeps a mother rotating and spinning around on cloud nine because she can now sit back and sometimes just watch all that hard work of action just demonstrate its motion all around Mom. This watched behavior will always keep that happy smile ☺ on Mom's beautiful face, seeing those results of progress, as well as seeing how her daughter may be even better at doing other tasks than her mom!

That's right, I said it! Better at certain tasks than you, Mom. Mothers, don't hate. It's perfectly okay for a daughter to have gifts that her mother may not have, or even okay to have skills, being without fault or defect. Remember we are all entitled to divine given gifts from our beautiful loved Creator! This is what makes you special. The secret is for mothers and daughters to claim this and, most certainly, do everything in their given power to accept their gifts and use all their given might and strength to make these gifts manifest, as well as develop them on an everyday basis. This practice of art and discipline will only open your mind and spirit to view and see that there really is no room for jealous behavior and suspicious conduct of rival energy. Your focus is and only should flow from yourself—from your own energy, not transformation onto others, all due to envious and jealous conduct.

A mother and daughter cannot win in this type of behavior. All it does is tear you down as a person, which does nothing for you, keeping both mother and daughter at zero—a distraction as to having a constant flow that I like to call a breakdown structure where no one ends up as a winner. It's a no-good thing, a wrong behavior. A mother and daughter who know how special their bond of unity is will not act and conduct themselves in any such way of conduct management, which is why this is one formula that always makes a mother and daughter special.

Mother's Day is a very special day—a celebration for all mothers all over the world to be recognized and praised for all their beautiful work of creation and of birth-giving, caring and sharing, and of touching so many lives. On that particular day, any public restaurant and eating place is always crowded. So many who love and cherish their mother are showing their appreciation for a mother's all-year-long sacrifice of dedication and truly hard work. So many wonderful daughters who show up and take their mothers out to enjoy a special brunch on that special day, all the beautiful cards that mothers give out to their mothers, letting their moms know how wonderful of them for always being there for much strong care, so much laughter and fun just shared . . .

There is so much happening on that special day. Just watch the mothers wearing their beautiful hats of all colors, daughters dressed at their best, showing how unique it is to have a mom. As for myself, walking around on Mother's Day, there is just so much love and happy energy flowing through the air. The warmth of high radar love is just really, really turned up on Mother's Day. This day will always be a day of celebration that we all will cherish. Daughters love to give back to their moms to show them just how much strong care they have for them on this special day. I sometimes like to even think back as to how I would always do my best as a child to figure out how to get and give my mother a gift. Even if I had no money to purchase her a gift, I would always make and design her a card, and my mom would always be so happy and share that the thought is what counts—and no matter, just writing and sharing this moment is just so touching and rewarding. It makes me think about how special my relationship was with my mom when she was living on earth. Now she is in heaven, enjoying the spiritual world.

Just thinking about her brings my energy up so high. Yes, my mother did prepare me to be a strong, determined woman. That itself is, no doubt, a special bond that I will carry always for her. That love and warmth for my mom in my heart forever lives on. So you see, there is just so much worldly thanks to give and send out about mothers and daughters' relationships. I can remember very clearly as of now how my father would always say and share with me how important it was for him to see and watch my mother and I get along the right way as mother and daughter. If there were any animosity or resentment of any kind of ties, my dad would put a stop to all that could turn into an argument and say, "You only get one mommy!" And when my dad would share that, I would just look at him for such a very long time, so speechless, because I knew he was making so much common sense. It was true. You only come into this world through your mother, which is why that statement always was held close to my father's heart. And this is why I listened closely to the hidden meaning in the words of my father. And as I write more and more, wisdom is traveling down onto paper . . . many, many reasons as to why a mother-and-daughter relationship is just so unique and special.

My mother would always do her best to uphold what she would like to quote "uphold the standards." She knew that a mother must practice having standards. She also understood how I was watching her and observing all the different tasks and things she would do and perform, not to mention my dad was always watching her and paying attention to how my mom would do things in and around the house. My mom knew having daughters was something special and that there were lots of duties with standards above and all around her divine assignment.

So, as of today, I write for the Creator to share all about what makes a mother and daughter special. The more I live life and behave gratefully for life, I truly do understand such joy and how special it really is to have a daughter. It empowers me to keep making efforts at doing what's right and to keep helping and assisting my daughter on her day-to-day journey in life, showing her the odds and ends of life. My daughter does make her own decisions, but nevertheless, if she does need or asks me for some guidance, I am present to help her and share with her what I think she should do and what's of really best for her interests.

Yes, I do let it be known to my daughter that I think of her as someone who is special in our home; however, at the same time, I do let her know that there are strong haters out in the world who don't want her to ever know, or dare to think, one thought about being special. I think I will always feel as though I should give my daughter a heads-up on certain things I know. There are certain situations she will have to find out on her own one day, and I am okay with this happening just for one certain fact: I have taught her well. What she will know and truly believe is that no matter what, her mom always showed her real special love and care.

Keeping Negativity out of Bonding

Can we talk about keeping negative bonding out? First, what does *negative* mean? Let us define this depressing word! *Negative*: "marked by denial, or refusal; showing a lack of something suspected or desirable; less than zero; having more electrons than protons; having light and shadow images reversed." In other words, or other ways of saying, it is straight up nothing good or right and nothing positive to say.

Have you ever been around that type of person who just doesn't have anything good to say? Their conversation just equals plain out zero—nothing right to say, nothing good to say! Well, I am here to inform you, when you recognize this behavior in front of you, or staring right at you or standing right at your doorstep full-pledged ready to get it going, get it started or, as the young ones like to put it: get it popping. Hold up your bright, bold red stop sign! I am not having it any better way to confront this matter; straight up, I am not having it!

A mother and daughter know what is best for their interests is to soul heartly not allowing anyone know one to put and bring negativity around them and on to their heart. Negativity and negative bonding will really destroy a mother-and-daughter bond. We are talking about a long, stretched-out motion of so much confusion until a mother-and-daughter bond will be, and become, so jammed up in the area of confusion. The best way to explain it is backed up, jammed up in traffic. It will be, and become, just so hard and difficult to move forward and go faster in both lives—the beautiful mother, as well as the daughter. We're talking about straight up stuck so hard, I mean very complex psychological problems—an energy, a motion of so much complexity that is just not the right beat to take on and move to this crooked motion.

I am going to say it, speak on it real loud in a real for-sure way as if I am a blimp up in the air as the light constantly blinks: "Keep negative bonding out!" It is just a down way of thinking. It's not going to take you anywhere if anything. What it really will do is rob you of all your vitality and life-force energy. So why let this waste of thought's destructive motion take you and bring you into discussion of what I like to call zap, take my energy. No way. No, no. Don't accept this. Don't allow it. Don't let it happen. Decline to this of a turn, or slope of downward wane. Refuse this way of talk. Don't accept this waste, this lower state of descending. It will not only tear down and bring a mother-daughter bond to straight zero—this lower state, or level of thinking, will war with your family level of thinking and downright destroy it generation from generation, back to back. It will most certainly destroy it—and I mean really tear you down, leaving you with zero sanity.

Be strong, stand up firm, and don't allow anyone to get away with turning your mother-and-daughter relationship into a negative bonding factory! Don't allow your heart of your center of home to be and become manufacturing to take place. Don't let this behavior become a way of being built up in you, or inside your home if it's taking place in your life as I write of it now! Stop it. You will not get too far with this motion. It's like trying to drive a car and there is no fuel, no gas, in the car. It's just not going to happen.

My mom would always remind me that there is a price to wear the crown. As I grew more in gaining understanding and wisdom, I now understand what she wanted me to start understanding—which meant most things in life are really not free, and most of the time, if it is free, there is some sort of attachment to it. What my mother wanted me to see and understand is when you wake up in the morning, don't be and don't think negative. Keep negative energy and negative action out your heart and life. It's a choice; you have divine rights to think and be positive. You can do that.

There is and there will be sometimes all sorts of negative situations going on and around you; however, as mother and daughter, it is not mandatory of being in the realm of participation. I know sometimes observational research is a must, just because it allows you to see what you need to see and stay away from what's wrong. Very true, however, the fact remains that you can protect that bond of pure spirit in your heart, although you must be, or become, responsible in a certain way. Just so you can become very sensitive to listen and hear that whispering voice of good, right behavior, keeping negativity out of your bond of respect that a mother and daughter have for themselves. This will become a motion of second nature just because there is just so much sometimes in the world—so many and many, many different ongoing situations of negativeness, there is so much negative bonding, so much of wrong negative conversation, until seeing this motion of action will and only just want to make you keep soul searching as to how to keep and stay out and away from giving in to this wrong, backward rhythm of results. That's why walking and talking about some of the wonderful and different tasks of things that have been done is a great positive way of staying connected to positive bonding. It is also a way of receiving reassurance and confidence that you can accomplish and will get what needed to be done in a positive motion and rhythm of positive action. You will gain strength and lots of courage, the ability to conquer fear and all that despair that negative puppets like to throw your way, if given any reason or doorway of entrance for doing so.

I think it's very healthy for a mother and daughter to take long walks together. It's real good for the pulse of each to really calm down and just see what's really taking place in their lives at that second with regard to seeing what the future holds and the plan of figuring out the calculations as to that golden question: what's next? Yes, sometimes what's next can really be a scary question, just because sometimes we simply really just don't know. And yes, it's okay not to know. When you know you don't know, it is okay to sit down. Sit still. Meditation is a good way to find out what it is you do need to know.

Meditation is a very good source for a mother and daughter to build their bond strong together. So many don't understand the power of bonding in the correct way. This right way of bonding will do the magic of keeping negative, bad bonding out. This is true and most for certain. Staying active, practicing a lifestyle of action, will keep a mother and daughter very grounded and very centered every day with regard to what's really right and best for them both. Every day, there will be a different task or performance expected from them. However, knowing and keeping the art of negative lifestyle out will only make it much easier for being able to take on and not let fear be an obstacle of standing in divine way, or opposing in any way of trying to bring you down, snatch you down, or tear you down in any way. Of course, the light of a positive bulb will act in your favor, staying and remaining in your realm of being and doing.

Positive tasks will box negative rhythm down. That is right: box that negative rhythm right on down. There is just no room for growth if you allow the fuse of a negative light to activate motion and rhythm to your life and in your daughter's life. The bond of negativity will destroy. It will bring in so much letdown energy, you will be moving around in such a way of so much fear. You will not only turn on yourself, you will cave in and turn completely inward toward yourself and your own actions. It will become so much of a serious strain to get work and things down the right and correct way.

As you can see, it is and will be a serious cost to be made for allowing negative bonding to wear and tear down your heart. I like to call it not knowing how to make right, good, sound choices, which is very important throughout your entire life. Knowing how to think properly for a mother and daughter is just so important. A mother and her daughter both must know how to keep that iron gate of protection around their hearts. And the gate comes with a key as well and, to think about it further, an alarm system around it as well.

Now why am I giving this by way of example? Because negativity wants a bond bad. I mean very, very bad. And if divine protection is not already around your bond when it tries to show up to kick you down, before you know it, that weak start-up conversation that gets nowhere goes nowhere once in. It's going to do what it is good at doing: downright destroy. So this is why that need for an alarm system around your heart is a must. Keeping positive control like positive patrol around the heart is so much needed in and for the time of day we live in. It's almost like having a hall pass. I think we all can relate to and remember those days in high school when we needed that permission slip, or that hall pass, to walk around school campus. Without it, you would get in trouble. Well, now that I am an adult, I know what to call that trouble. Negative bonding negative attack straight up on you and bow and arrow right through you. So you see, this is why it's a must that what I write be told to readers out there in the world of beautiful creation.

Remember to swing up and practice boxing back. Don't fall down; box back. Or if you do fall down, remember you can always get back up. Don't just stay down there. Remember the force of negativity enjoys seeing you squirm at staying down and not knowing how to stand up and gain that motion of strength and force of might from the Almighty. Once again, all else that's weak and dull don't have no meaning of life force anyway. The force of Satan, most of the time, is a big letdown anyway; so therefore, stay strong and centered at keeping your mother-and-daughter bond in the realm of being kind to one another, as well as loyal and operating in the realm of positive thinking and right-willed support!

Negative bonding is a waste of time and always will be; its motion is of so much drain. Why give it one cent of your valued time—of letting it in, or of concern? The power of the mother-and-daughter bond is just so and too special to worry or care at all how to please crazy, negative, fake bonds. A mother has more and other sorts of goodwill tasks to do and perform versus all else no going anywhere rhythm and motion. Remember life is beautiful and made to be enjoyed—not a big letdown of nothing, or zero. Always know and understand that's just what negativity wants to do, and that's what negative bonding is all about.

Now I am going to talk about negative bonding reaction. As of right now, you're sharing to yourself within: "I am a positive person. I am just so high-spirited." So positive until negative energy just don't fade you, or just can't catch your fade as the young ones quote on quote like to share out in the streets. However, how do you respond to negative reaction? Yes, you do have some people who just love to get a negative response from someone who is positive, or who has a positive mother-daughter bond relationship—so what's really going on when we talk about negative reaction? Yes, now I am bringing this discussion about negativity straight as clear and right up front home. I am talking about if you have control when negative energy catches on to you and does its best to knock you down; and sometimes, it just wants to seriously downright destroy you!

Queen Roshaunda has one question. How do you handle it, or how do you think it should be handled? Now this is very tricky, and it is almost like walking on needles. I will give you an example. Your teenage daughter may be around the age sixteen, and she does not come home. And to make this situation a little worse, you get a phone call that she is at that young male's house that you really know deep from within has no further interest or care in your daughter's further life as well! What do you do? You must admit, this is a high realm of negativity motion bonding—and yes, this force clearly knocks you straight to the ground. What do you do? How do you handle this?

From doing research, what I observed was what happened from most mothers behavior is going smooth off. I am talking about seriously blowing up, not knowing that somewhere on there behave know observation of seeing this coming and happening was on its way! So Mom totally explodes, and then what happens? Negativity you let it in, and now guess what? You have now been introduced to negativity bonding, and it's going to bloom like a beautiful flower in its worst way that you may in no way even think to imagine. All because your action was a reaction from negative motion. Don't bow into it or as what youngsters like to share: don't bow down to it because if done so, you are going to get zapped so far down, I only hope you will be able to swing back up. From a positive strictness with a solution that's positive to only help move negative out its way so you both can keep moving in positive rhythm and positive motion. Otherwise, the triple negative bond, it just gets worse—and that's what you do not want. Always use your heart, mind, and inner spirit when negative-reaction response comes your way, or shows up to visit you in an unwelcome manner. Please don't bite back or, I can share, don't just give in to it. Then you will really see it so clearly for what it really is.

Don't give in to competition or compete back with it, because that's all that it is and what it wants. Bottom line: remove from it quickly. And a better way to remove that situation is the example I gave about a mother's sixteen-year-old daughter going camping with your daughter to take a trip what's of most importance and what you really must do just block that open space in her life. And you get in that area of her life and cover it up until she can become responsible for covering that area up herself in positive light energy and positive focus. That way, negative bonding will bounce right off and will not be able to take down, or tear down, positive energy. Remember negative energy is all around, sometimes ready to strike at positive energy. However, positive energy is present and does live as well. Knowing this will, and can, make a mother-daughter relationship much, much better!

I like to always share that a mother-and-daughter relationship is very important and that there are just so many rewards when the strong determination of getting along is important and valued. There will be no hesitation and no doubt, or pause, about when to execute or carry out fully when to strike back and not let the negative bombard and get in and bond with that tear-down negativity force. It is so not worth it. Negative bonding is really nothing but a weak coward. It's almost like that person who walks around like a bully until, one day, that bully really meets their match. Sometimes all it takes for a person with stand-up power for themselves, and from then on, no more bullying goes on.

I shared that to say negative bonding is very similar in a way because once it knows that you're not going to give in to it and you seriously mean that you're not going to, it will not bring you that drama of its operation because seeing that it's not being tolerated is very clear in the realm of viewing and seeing sometimes in the life of a mother. Knowing that their feet must stand firm and remain grounded to what you say and mean, and that's just how it goes by example. When mothers behave and demonstrate this solid motion, it's only a normal reaction for a daughter, or daughters, to practice and demonstrate the same, exact behavior. This is just how it is in life; otherwise, there are no boundaries of control in your own life and all those areas of what you say and how you live your life.

Yes, it does take a lot of spunk and self-determination to live a boss-up lifestyle; however, the rewards and gifts are all so much of worthiness, not to even mention all the gifts that you attain to hold on throughout your day. And further, you are just so able to get so much of what you really want and need, the universe opens up in so many divine ways to serve you as well.

There are so many different, beautiful walks of life. When you keep negative bonding out of a mother-and-daughter relationship, you just keep right on moving, going up, living a lifestyle of real serious elevation—not to mention having fun but being responsible at the same time. As I like to quote it, "Let the love flow," and all else like hate have to plain right just step back—which I sometimes like to define that it has to get out of your way, or move out of the way. Not hard to understand, right? When a mother and daughter keep negative bonding out, they're both able to govern and, the way I see it and explain it, map quest their lives out every single day in control where they're going, and in terms of what they're doing and wanting to do and accomplish, but nevertheless in charge of who rolls in or who gets rolled over. To me, this is life. And really, there is just no other way to play if you can understand and relate.

My mother would always share that 10 percent of things and situations in your life are sometimes situations that happen and occur, and sometimes you just may not even see these events approaching—or you just have no control of what's happening. And the other 90 percent of your life is really what you make it to be or come about. I have lived for quite some time in my own eyesight to really believe what my mom shared to be of truth. I tell my daughter to always take control of creating her life and lifestyle in the order she wants it to be, and to take control. She knows it starts by keeping negative bonding out. This only will give you that sense of control you need and must have. So therefore, others have no control over running you and making your own decisions and choices. As Beyonce quoted in her 2013 song: "You can say to yourself I bow down to no one, except the one Almighty Creator who made me."

Sometimes it's just good for a mother and daughter to take a long, good Greyhound bus ride together, viewing and looking at nature together. It will help keep negative bonding out as well, being on the bus with others who mind their own minds and their own business. Everyone is really going somewhere that was their own plan of arrival, so therefore, being around focused ones pushes you back into focus of self. Although you're relaxing and enjoying the bus ride, you're very much focused on your inner realm of positive bonding. Most of time, it's quiet and a ride very much well worth the price of the ride. It's strongly recommended for a mother and daughter to get together, having as many different hobbies of fun as possible.

Remember your life is really made to be pretty much enjoyed, and to feel that joy of real accomplishment—laughter and real, true excitement. My mom would always say, "Let no one steal or rob you of your joy." Remember there are still those kinds of humans in the world we live around today who will just take and take from you, and if you're not on a constant stand at keeping negative bonding out and away and from around yourself and your lifestyle, the flood of negativity will be all around you to seriously zap you, and this is what you must not tolerate and allow. Remember, a mother-and-daughter bond must be made around positive missiles moving around in positive motion, reaping all the rewards and benefits due for having, just because of making a rightful stand for living life positively and not allowing negative bonding to come in to drown and flood your mind and lifestyle in despair and want and lack.

In life, it is very wise to understand we have to make choices and know how to make right choices that are really best for our lives. Keeping your mind positive is possible when negative seeks a way in. You can check that thought right away, override it with a positive thought. Do not allow negativity to reach at you, or obtain you. Stop it, check it, and you will see how it will bounce right off and away from your thinking. Negativity is like a heavy weight. It will lay heavy on your heart and seriously tear you down. No one needs all this wear and tear on and around their heart and on their mental mind. It's not fun at all. Your heart should feel as though light feathers are over it. You should be able to move around as light as a feather. Another way of explanation is some people will try to enter your life and bring you heavy boxes on your heart and smash them feathers. This is why a mother and daughter have to be, or become, very aware. Just don't sit around and not watch and observe what's entering around, or what's trying to get in and at you.

Observation is a serious must. Mother and daughter have to show strong teamwork at protecting themselves and their environment of where they're at. This is very important at all times, staying disciplined at keeping negative energy out. Remember negative energy is poison. It is a vim energy that likes to avenge, exonerate, justify it's okay to bring in poison. What's not good for you should never be welcome.

Make an art of keeping away from venom. I know poison is secreted by animals out in the wild jungle; however, it's time to really accept that some adults sit around and act worse than animals and look to use words of poison that destroy good energy and self-esteem—which is why these adults that do behave in this manner are so much worse than animals, because the animal is who it should be, or simply doing what it does.

Some environments are just really, really negative until, in some cases, you really have to make a strong presence of being as to the fact that you own that environment, just to let negativity know. Knock it off—bounce off, and get back! Positive runs the show, letting negative know your time is just so limited. No one or nobody has a right to try to control another human being by executing and carrying out negative motion of friction. You have to be as a gatekeeper who just keeps it out: one who doesn't let it in. As far as I see it, this is just the new way of living the good life, being and staying positive and keeping straight negativity out. I like to quote it: exemption staying exempt for free going know where BS.

Always strive to own your own It is no one else's. It belongs to you: your self! What I like to call it me, myself, and I—your own unique bill of rights of sale (ha-ha ☺ = smile). Remember when you're just taking a walk down the street and hear negative bonding, sometimes it will try to approach you. You don't have to let it in. It can try to get you all turned up, and twist it up. Keep at, keep it moving. Don't allow it to ride your life, or lifestyle. Dust it off your shoulders and keep right on along being positive. Just remember there are many rewards in a mother-daughter bond when your focus is to stay positive. It is just the way to live your life—the way to go when disappointment shows up at times. You both will know just how to keep it going and keep moving in your strong ways of remaining positive.

There are lots of great people who have made it a serious, conscious effort every day of their beautiful lives to get up to be and do positive motion every day in and throughout the days in their lives. Beyonce is so positive, and she and her mother are just great, awesome role models as to what a mother-daughter's positive bond is all about, and that is doing: doing what you love to do. And what it boils down to it is taking care of what I like to call business matters, making that mean long, money if you know what I mean my readers ☺. You're able to think so much better when you keep negative bonding out. You only will start to really see all the options you have at making life greater and better for self.

One's self should and always be of your best concern for how you should set out to make every day worth living to your greatest satisfaction—at least at doing most of what it is you want and will do when your mind is clear as a crystal ball sparkling clean. The fun of it all is keeping a positive mind-set and eliminating negative thoughts, or I could just say casting down negative thoughts of wild hard-core imagination. I must admit negative imagination can be a dangerous swing at the beautiful mind; however, we don't have to let those thoughts of take-down in. We all have the right to take in fresh, clear thoughts of ideas, so let's claim it, mothers and daughters: positive bonding, keeping the negative and negativity bonding out of our hearts and minds. Let's make our lives what we want them to be and what they should be. You don't have to give up. You can keep on galloping like a horse does, just looking beautiful and happy for being what it is—a horse. I like to think of how delicate horses really are, but at the same time, they are very grounded and, for certain, looking positive—as we should always be, mothers and daughters!

Remember, learn to own your destiny. What I mean by this is take control of what you want to happen in your life, and just go right on and do just that—live your destiny to the fullest of lots of excitement and enjoyment. Own your walk; own your divine walk of life. You, mothers and daughters, are so worthy of all this happening and existence of your own happy reality. When you keep bringing positive bonding on negative bonding, it just has to leave no room for it. It has to just stay right on out! You exercise mentally at keeping the negative out of your mother-and-daughter bonding, and you box mentally at handling all those negative thoughts that like to creep in and tear you down.

Mental positive push-ups are such a must; doing mental push-ups is what I like to call upliftment thoughts transforming your thoughts in an upward motion of positive thinking, giving you rewards always just because you have trained your thoughts to be obedient to positive frequency. Positiveness does have a frequency, and it will pick up a signal of your vibration, just like negative will tear you down and will vibe on you when you're not aware of just how negative does work. I have said so much about keeping negative bonding out in my closing of this chapter. Just remember that you are just too awesome to have to deal and take on negative bonding. Stay blessed and remember: you don't have to let stress in. Peace.

Smile

Joy

Laughter

Happiness

Thoughtfulness

Mother-Daughter-Bond
Emotions in Check

Roller coaster of love, say what? Ha-ha! I know some are saying what is she talking about? And then some would say "I remember that song!" It is a song that I would jam to get my groove on. Well, let me stop! Let's get right to the point why I shared Roller Coaster of Love.

Okay, how many of us can admit that emotions sometimes can spin around in a vortex, confusing most of us. Emotions out of control . . . Sometimes when they're out of control and not in balanced motion and rhythm, they can and will seriously destroy you and most certainly stop you from doing what you should do from a logical stance. Emotions sometimes can scoot over, squeeze in, and remove logic until we are totally operating and thinking from crazed, insane emotions—a lack of understanding totally not aware and not knowing of what the *H* is really going on. This is very dangerous for a mother and daughter. A mother and daughter are supposed to have these emotions seriously in check just so happiness, fun, and joy can be present at least of making every day to make sure that their emotions are in check. What I am quoting is proper order of conduct, making certain that you are in control of your emotions; your emotions should not be controlling your being.

A real, true mother knows how to behave and act in the present moment with her daughter. She knows how to act, and she sees clearly at all times how she has to teach her daughter to keep her emotions in check. Otherwise, she knows if she does not—welcome to a world of problems, wasting of time, and of not knowing how to keep fools out of divine life! Let me explain when and what can happen when fools are let in with foolish, silly thinking—different things and situations which are just all wrong with ill, bad behavior.

A fool is a *herum spielen zum*, I like to say—one who simply just does not think about self or anyone in any particular situation, not caring of what is just downright just act in and on any given topic only done from emotions of not being controlled and running their decision making process from a rhythm of not thinking whatsoever!

Now a daughter knows too that she does not want to see her mom act with emotions not controlled properly in a logical fashion. A daughter knows her chances of right, proper, correct guidance is going to be totally out of existence. A daughter expects her mom to have her emotions in check to always help and still be able to give her mom real supreme guidance. It has nothing to do with knowing right from wrong; that's a taught past of lessons already learned. We're talking about emotions, knowing what, when, why, who and who should have control and knowing how to separate the two, feelings, or logic and at high level of thinking combinement of both energies in harmony to produce the right result. This is what a daughter expects from her mother; take it or leave it alone.

Have you ever witnessed on looking or seeing, or observation, how humans sometimes can act when their emotions are out of check and out of total control? I know we all have at least seen one individual throughout our lives who behaved in this out-of-control motion. It's just a crying shame to watch. It's not even pleasant to see children throwing indecent tantrums, let alone an adult—and not to mention, men out of control of how their emotions work and operate are just downright dangerous. So as a mother-and-daughter example, mothers and daughter, we must give a showing of how we can manage them and keep them so much in divine check! Otherwise, you will find yourself in so many different confrontations with so many unwanted situations. Remember you want happy emotions, and you really do want to have them in control to reap all your divine benefits that are due to you in life. You just have to understand, mothers and daughters of the world, you are somebody—and that somebody is a great human being who deserves to really have control over their mind and state of being. This is a for-sure statement of unity with your mind.

In it for myself to be a born writer, I have to have control over my emotions; otherwise, I couldn't or would not even take the time to write. So you see, I to must make every day an effort at exercising control of my beautiful emotions as well! I remember one day walking out of Albertson Market, and I heard this woman screaming and hollering out loudly, upset that her taxicab had not shown up. She was so upset and hurt by the fact that she had to wait so long. There was nothing she could find to do but scream out loud and convey to others how upset she was, not knowing she was just using her emotions in a bad, uncontrolled way. This woman, at least, had to be around fifty years of age, all of no control of self, or her mind emotions no knowledge of ever practicing to keep those emotions in check, as well as keeping her divine self in check.

I do believe a lot of this starts from not growing up in practice of how to keep your emotions under control, although in life certain circumstances and situations can happen that will change one's life on a day to day base. However it's a must for a mother and daughter to make a showing together of how to keep their emotions in check. This really is the only way of having control to make things go your way in your life; otherwise, being defeated will happen much of the time, and no one wants that to keep happening, all due to blowing up out of control. Remember, you want to know how to handle your situations. Knowing the power of management always helps a mother and daughter manage their bond of emotions in check. There is just no other way to do this, the exercise of control.

As we all can see, this situation—from a clear perspective—if not done, you will suffer later through the years in your life, and this is just what you do not want to happen in life. There are enough to take on, but nevertheless, when your emotions are in check, things will go a lot smoother for you. You want more of the happy, good experiences in your life. There is about 20 percent that you cannot control from happening; the other percentage you want to have control over, for your life. This way, you won't feel as if your life and lifestyle are getting away from you. Remember structure is something one must remain determined to stay in; if you're not determined, you will feel as if you are unable to create and have your life and lifestyle the way you want it, and how you want it to go.

Remember you make it happen, mothers and daughters. No one else does it for you; you have to get up and go do this. Otherwise, you will sit and think others are going to make it happen for you. Trust me, they're not. You have to kick wrong out and do your best not to let wrong thoughts come into your beautiful mind and dominate your thoughts. Don't have it, and don't allow it. Stay in the mental realm of emotions in check, and this will only keep producing a powerful mother-daughter bond that will be everlasting on earth.

Always know a mother-daughter bond is really special and should be guarded in its high honor of respect anyway, and one of the ways of respecting the bond is having and keeping those emotions in check. Remember emotions are there and can and will rise up in some similar situations, and sometimes in different situations—however, one or the other will know to let expression take place in a divine civilized way, just so self-control can remain a strong factor in the equation of expression.

Have you ever witnessed a mother and daughter, or a mother with her daughter, and they're just going at it twenty-four-seven, just downright arguing to their highest degree until it's just a crying shame just seeing how this energy will just escalate can get higher and higher and go so up until it's just viewed in a way until coming down in a reasoning, logical way, it's almost of not being possible for notification. This is just bad behavior to see, or witness; however, I have seen it, and I am quite sure some of my readers have seen this as well. These feelings—what we like to call our emotions—if given the right proper attention too, we are the ones who can have right, proper control over them. Remember to always not let your emotions control you. It is so hard to operate in this world and everyday life and not have these emotions in order and in check. You want to live life and enjoy life; so therefore, we must keep our emotions up under management control!

Good energy is what you want to send out, and vibe out, at others—not loose, unwrapped, out of control over those emotions. People will see it and recognize you coming and go hard, aim at tearing you down. Sometimes your family and some others will delightfully enjoy tearing down that mother-daughter bond. A mother-and-daughter bond has to have high regards in knowing how to keep both emotions in check and so much self-control. A lot of times, people will try and test you just to see if they're of gaining, any luck in your areas of categorizing you any way. I mean, you have a percentage of people who will try to come into your life and do just that: push those emotional buttons just to see you go haywire and lose total control. And once you make this kind of showing, guess what? Their permanent behavior will be this way around you, just because you didn't have your emotions in check when the buttons were pushed.

Stay in your mother-and-daughter bond; keeping it in check is just so important. Happy, controlled emotions will take you in so many doors, wonderful doors of life, attaining and having what it is you want. Let's talk about what actually happens when a mother and daughter have their emotions in check when they're out in public, as well as when they're invited to different social events! Lots of fun excitement transcends of inspiration become an automatic forming habit; there is such a rhythm of good habit.

A habit is defined as "rhythm of doing something over and over." However, in this case of senior, this is practice of good habit. Both mother and daughter will enjoy having such a good time because their emotions are downright in check. Observation and what should be noticed and taken in will not be missed whatsoever; both will be operating what I sometimes like to call hard-core love of unity, just because those emotions are so much in check in the right way.

Have you ever been to any social barbecue events? Lots of fun is going down; people are having blasts of fun. Some are jumping in the big swimming pool, having a blast, just downright having fun—and then checkmate. There's that group of females that are just present at the event. Don't have a clue of knowing, really should only be there to have fun, and before you know it, they're watching and observing this one group that are enjoying themselves, or just having an extra amount of fun and *boom*! The group of these females who don't have those emotions in check crash the fun, knock the party out of right rhythm all down because of not knowing. They have not been taught how to really just keep those emotions in check. And the group that's enjoying themselves, having a blast, if they're not careful now, all or some will be thrown out of right rhythm if the situation is not handled correctly and carefully, all due to that group whose emotions weren't in check before arriving.

It's sad to speak on this subject in this way; however, it is really true and present if you take notice and just look around and view for one second or moment. I suggest when you give a fun event, there should be a sign posted: KEEP EMOTIONS IN CHECK. Put it right at the door! It might not be the whole, entire solution to this situation; however, it does play some part in helping the situation from going out of control—or one could just say losing balance and control.

When you think about emotions, you understand what psychology means: "science of mind and mental behavioral aspect," as of an individual's sometimes distorted, out-of-control mental thinking. Now just for a second, really think about that group that showed up at the barbecue who didn't have those emotions in check—and didn't really make out, or understand, their arrival was there to have fun, not crash the party. Emotions out of control, really out and all over the place, so bad and ruined until you cannot even think in sections what I like to call emotions all over the place, like a plate of spaghetti all over the place.

When you think in sections, it's like slots knowing when and where something should be given and placed at its proper time of satisfaction. Example: at the dinner table, you would not sit your shoes on top of the table. Your nature would communicate with you. It's the wrong place for those shoes, and you would know immediately that those shoes should remain on the floor or in the closet—not on the table. This is why emotions must be kept in check in their proper right place of how we think and are controlled by our act of duties. Although I have witnessed seeing a young woman put her shoes on top of the table, a perfect example, her emotions had to be in and all over and scattered in her thinking to do such a thing and dare not to think anyone was not going to say something. That wasn't the case; someone did share something. So you see, the more our emotions are in check, the less we don't have to hear others tell us what we do not want to hear. When your energy is all over the place and not controlled rightly, your emotions most certainly will not be in check.

A mother and daughter must operate in the realm of rational thinking. What I like to call those emotions in check—you will be able to laugh more and smile more when your emotions are in check.

People will have a much harder time at making you feel and become upset. Your energy force field will be channeled more in the right way. You will know when it is just time to practice patience where as getting disturbed and being disturbed because of not being able to conduct others' motion, or your own motion at all first place rhythm. Sometimes you will just have to accept the facts and agree sitting down in sit still motion is the way to go.

There will be times when others just are not and will not move as fast as you want them to, or would like them to. However, when your emotions are in check, it does make any given situation much easier to deal with, better from a mentally strong psychological stance. Emotions all over the place that are not checked are not good. I mean every day in our lives, we are so most of certain responsible how our day is to go. The more a mother and daughter keep those emotions in check, the better of attainment will be and become. Most humans want to have and attain every day anyway; however, if your emotions are not in check, it will be a lot harder to see your way clearly in having or attaining what you want.

A lot of times, the items to want are really having an attraction toward you anyway. The better you are in control of your emotions being in check, you will have the tools to get them. Remember good attraction is what you want, not to mention drain. You do not have to allow others to come in and drain you, mothers and daughters. You keep your peace and keep moving around in mental peace, which I sometimes like to say emotions in check. It is also good for a mother to say morning affirmations, "I will keep my emotions in check!" And for daughters, as well. It is so important to quote the morning affirmation: "Emotions in check today." You will see how much smoother and easier your day will go. Not only smoother, your perception will become so much clearer than everyone's.

Needs are to make things and situations better; it is just of being able to do it. Living in the knowing and knowing how to live in your own power as of doing as of right now very much of importance. Always know you really don't want your emotions to rule you; you want them in check! Not to travel through your logic of one's reasoning. One of the key ingredients to controlling emotions is having proper submission. We all must learn and practice every day throughout our lives how to submit. You have to submit to yourself to not allow emotions to control you or to take you down. Stop allowing emotions to govern and control your mind. Don't come undetached, or I could shove. Don't come unglued. Remember, you want to remain and stay glued, keeping a right state or frame of mind!

Walking around feeling unglued and acting unglued will keep you from making progress. You will start to feel as though you are becoming more stuck. This is only going to produce ill feelings. No one wants to put a claim on ill, bad feelings. You want good, right positive feelings—those happy feelings. And the righteous claim of good feelings is through proper, right submission.

Knowing how to use the keys of submission conduct will take you so much further and forward into your future to come remember it's about a mother and daughter making progress, not digressing or wandering from the main subject, which is mother and daughter remaining and keeping control, overall having a balanced bond to keep their emotions in check! I see, too many times, circumstances and lots of different situations where mothers and daughters lose so much self-control while out in public, all from their emotions not being in check.

Yes, we all must strive to be, and remain, as centered as possible. There really is no need to hit and sock your daughter in the back at Target department store in front of lots of people who are just strangers and now being onlookers. This only happens from emotions not being in check. There is no explanation for no-control emotions that I like to share emotions running around inside all over the place, not being in a sane, controlled environment. This type of out-of-control behavior must be worked on. Do not make this a brand-new way for a lifestyle. You want it controlled and to be much better for yourself, as well as for both mother and daughter. Remember, in life, the sky is the limit. And in order to really reach the sky, rule number 1 is it helps and makes such a big difference when your emotions are in check.

Sometimes if you just listen and observe what words are being spoken by others, it's just so many loose words that do not make any good sense. It all stems from those emotions running around inside, out of harmony with their sound logic, the reasoning part of self which is such of not good crazy emotions really will only get you nowhere you want to get from A to B in life. It's not fun to be stuck at A, and what makes it worse—you're trying to move off from A, and you're stuck with no progress. This is so bad for growth and progress. You want motion from point A to point B.

A mother and daughter should live a good lifestyle—a lifestyle of having control over themselves, not letting their emotions dictate how their lives should be lived. When you allow emotions to dictate or control your life, they block out your good reasoning and sound judgment, and that is what you do not want to become a part of. It only leads your life to a blank and empty spot, and it sort of opens room for distorted thinking to get in and have its way with you. You don't want that to happen. Remember you want to keep those emotions in check just alone so you can see clearly and hear and listen to your inner self guide and instruct you.

When your emotions are all over and around the place, it makes it that much harder to hear your inner self and do right by making wise, sound decisions of reasoning or choice. What you do not want is to be controlled by and from inner confusion. You want clarity. When a mother and daughter have inner clarity together, you both gain such an inner strength of accomplishment together as mother and daughter. Mom and daughter both will know how to swing upright to bring about the desired strong-willed goals. This is all in and from the keeping of mother-and-daughter-bond emotions in check. Yes, it does take a certain amount of strength to accomplish this new way of thinking; however, it can be done. Seeing your blessed rewards will only motivate you more and more to have and attain a controlled way of thinking.

Sometimes in life, there are certain situations we must and have to accept, and that is having control over our minds and our beautiful lives. We have to get up and do just what we know we must do to stop all these emotions and out-of-control behavior. Get up and just go do it. The more we see good results, this will give us fuel to keep on succeeding.

Being able to keep your emotions in check, making sure they're not going haywire and all out of control is success in itself as well. Every day you can walk outside your home and view and see so much of how so many people battle every day keeping those emotions in check— that's why it does really start at home with mothers and daughters keeping their emotions in check. Remember, in life, you want peace, not war. And peace starts from within, just like war starts from within. It's best to choose peace from within, and all else will start to fall right in line for you. I like to call it the harmony of emotions being in check. The more a mother and daughter practice the art of emotions being in check, feelings will not be able to overdominate you when you should not be making a decision based on feelings. Your sound reasoning will override those feelings anyway, and most certainly, you both will be better at completing difficult tasks that will likewise require you to have those emotions in check.

Sometimes you will have to be regimented, very rigidly organized for control to make orderly, sound choices and decisions. However, it can and will be done when you have understanding as to the importance for all and of every need that is of so much importance. Emotions in check will force a mother and daughter to take care of business. There is just no way of escaping the everyday task of taking care of business. Business is one of the first power laws in life that must be practiced, which is all the reason as to why emotions must come under control and be in check. Doing business with people and communicating the business language requires self-control and self-discipline anyway, so why not keep and maintain those emotions in check? Really, there's no choice; it's a must to keep lifestyle emotions in check.

Remember there will be some who are just downright adversary. wanting to make you lose control and not have your emotions in check. You will be able to see who these individuals are, and you will be extra equipped in all areas of dealing with those who will show up just to take you from your self-control. By practicing the art of keeping emotions in check, you will help and immediately show, by your own demonstration to others: "I will not allow you to make me lose my self-control." Your showing will be "my emotions are in check." Others will also start to see the effort you're making, of how you are making sure those emotions or protected.

Mother and daughter have to keep and have structure around themselves and their emotions. There is no escape. You just have to stay at it, use strong effort at practicing this task of awakening energy. You must do your best at being and becoming better every single day of your life so that you can see clear and truly understand who you are at being a mother or at being a daughter. You must strive at knowing self. It will keep you in the gates of doing what you want to do, and you will also know what you should stay away from. Proper submission is really a strong key at having control over those emotions. Submission in itself will control those emotions. Proper, right submission will stop wild out-of-control emotions right in their tracks.

Have you ever been in a room or situation, around a lot of different personality types, and there is that one person who just talk-talk-talk-talks too much in a way where they're just telling all their downright business, sharing private information, discussing topics that should not be shared so openly in a public setting. And most of the people who are in the room will share among each other what's wrong with that individual. Why are you sharing all your personal information?

I am here to share with you, this behavior all stems and comes from not having those emotions in check. This is why it's so important for a mother and daughter to have their emotions in check and not go wild, crazy, or out-of-control. If this be the case of those emotions really out of control, there really is going to be a serious problem. Emotions being out of check can and will be very, very dangerous. This is why proper submission is very important. It helps you keep emotions in check. Remember, as mother and daughter, you really just want to move forward. So when you do see out-of-control behavior, you will remember it's okay to use your listening skills in a way of practicing obedience. Listening is very important in a lot of certain ways. It's just how it is sometimes. If we would all just sit still and listen, things would—and will—most certainly reveal and show themselves. This practice of action really does help get the results that is of seeking because of want.

Keeping emotions in check will keep you connected to your divine self. You really do have to be cautious and very selective whom you would be around and go around with. The reason I share this is some people who may feel as if you should not be around them will automatically cause and set your off button to lose your self-control, just for their purpose to see you lose that self-control so your emotions can go haywire so you will experience lack of control. Remember, birds of a feather flock together: meaning those alike sip from the same cup. As for those sipping from the wrong cup, they are only going to find themselves drinking from a cup of poison, which is just really not going to be a good drink. So therefore, all I am saying is watch close-range and, most certainly, pay attention to whom you roll around with—or one might say who you are around. The more a mother and daughter practice keeping those emotions in check your self-radar will be and become so much stronger in being able to have discernment as to not being able to be pulled in by the wrong ones who want to take you down that wrong path, just to witness and see you lose control and feel satisfied that your emotions were not in check.

We all know how important it is to do what's said from within. When emotions are out of check and running extremely wild, how can you get it done? What's of importance, your energy will be so blocked from many different ways from within, which will only lead to not knowing how to submit. It's just not going to get done right if your submission is off. Being around wrong folks who do not have your entrance in caring will only tamper and make sure that your submission is off and of know sort of balance, which will be of a welcome giving those bad company ones all the benefit of doubt to destroy your emotions as well.

One way to avoid bad company is making sure you really do practice the art every day as a mother is at of keeping them emotions seriously in check and the same ordeal as daughters should keep those emotions in check so you can do things and enjoy your life as well. No one really wants to have those intense emotions all over the place. In life, you really do want to be able to follow through, carry out those rewarding tasks that are going to require some self-control. So why not have those emotions in check to gain self-control to do what's needed by you and what you want to do and accomplish?

Having an understanding of self is just so important sometimes. I will hear individuals say "I don't know myself. I am in a relationship with someone, and I don't really know myself and understand myself," or that having knowledge of themselves is such a foreign way for understanding to be present. That is such a bad way to live—not to understand who you are and know who you are. That's no fun, not good. You really do miss out in life when you do not know and understand self. Not knowing self really does and can lead to wasting your time with the wrong people, as well as allowing others to drain your valued time and energy as well. Keeping those emotions in check will teach you in a given way of having them in check and control to not going around those who just are downright set out to take your emotions down, and straight set out to disturb those emotions from being in check.

So remember, mothers and daughters, it's good every day to practice the power of staying focused so you can get and do what needs to be done, just so you can move on and keep moving toward what and where you're supposed to go. And I also will share in closing out this chapter, it is good as well to practice the art of sometimes standing still. This also helps at keeping those emotions in check, and it always makes it so much better when overlooking the ocean in a standing-still position, just to watch the motion and hear the sound of the ocean. It will help keep those emotions in check. The sound of the ocean will most definitely have checkmated those emotions.

Keeping Haters out of
that Divine Bond

Let's talk! I have a serious question to ask my readers. Do you think haters are real? Do haters really exist, or did your mother and father warn you to know that haters are real! Since I don't really know what you've been told—well, I am going to just say it. Haters are real! And guess what? Sometimes you will and can feel as if they're everywhere, ready to get it started at tearing down and destroying if they see that it is possible to get away with doing so.

Therefore, we must learn the art of keeping haters out of that divine bond a mother has with her daughter—or in some cases, daughters. Yes, there is a way to protect that divine bond. You can start by guarding your beautiful, pure heart. Learn to value your heart more. Make all possible extra efforts to keep away from what's not right and, most certainly, stay away from others' low talk of foolishness. You don't have to listen to foolish conversation. Your heart, as a mother, will become so much stronger when you decide to not allow bad, wrong, foolish poisons in your mind, heart, ears, and spirit. Your radar will be and become so extra strong, hate will become scared of you. Remember, hate don't even know why it hates sometimes. It's just confused, and the force field doesn't know what to do sometimes and doesn't have a clue where to go. Remember, hate cannot live in a genuine heart that's operating in love.

Love is powerful and will always do what it is best at: running out hate and keeping hate out. Daughters of the world, you must do the same task as well. Don't make contact with the negative ones. Keep them out. Stay away from the haters; keep them away and out of your life. Always remember, you don't need hate in your life—you only need love and truth. Remember, haters love to project their poison; however, you don't have to let that venom of bad poison in. And be aware it's a force that is real and out in the world. However, keep your divine self within you connected to love and nature and doing good deeds. When your energy is around hate, it will not be able to come through you. Don't be a vessel for hate, daughters. You want to be a vessel for love. You will enjoy your life so much better and get way much more done than those brainless haters.

Remember that haters' energy is all confused, messed up, and entangled in fear and starting trouble—just straight up miserable haters are those who like to bring you down to zero if there is a way to get away with it. This is why a mother and daughter must use their mighty power of strength to not let hate interrupt their divine bond of power. Keep them haters out; back them haters up. Showing love is here. Love is present in a divine, natural way. You can do it. You can keep the wrong ones out. You just have to keep doing right. It's almost as if you have Mace in your mind, and you press that spray button back up. And I am for real about you backing up, so for real until I press that red button until your eyes are bloodshot red from spray being in and out all through your eyes. As you can see, you have to swing out in a strong motion to keep that poison of hate away from the divine ones.

You really sometimes do have to mind your own business, which can mean it is just best to really stay in your own mind. It's just best to do your best every day to take care of your own personal business. A lot of times, when a mother or daughter go sticking their heads in others' business, it will cause so many different situations with many problems that will come along. And before you know it, the scent of hate is being released. And yes, hate is really a file-stiken scent. Love really don't want it around, trying to bring down the aroma of love, so this is why a mother and daughter must do their divine best to make extra effort to live a good, fun life and, at the same time, keep all that hate out of their lives, as well as keep haters from sneaking in and trying to move you off your path and take you from doing what you know you must do every day of your life.

Remember, haters cause trouble and, at the same time, start trouble and don't have any remorse of starting trouble and know carrying of what's so ever bringing divided and division of trouble and confusion in and all others environment and lifestyle. Remember always, mothers and daughters, do the things in life that bring you lots of joy. Keep on seeking lots of fun and laughter in your everyday life. Don't let haters get you down and bring you down. Remember, you don't have to claim fear; being bold and going to do what you want to do make life worth living every day. Haters will try to block that divine path that's good to seek. Just do it anyway, and life will always be so much joy and fun. To live and enjoy your life, you will not be afraid to do what you will need to do and want to do. You will just make it happen every day. Take that trip, take that cruise—it's always a good bonding day for a mother and daughter to take a cruise together. Lots of joy it brings to the soul, and there are so many good and wonderful things to tell and talk about.

The more a mother and daughter bond the right way together, the harder it is for haters to find their way in to cause havoc and problems. It's great to just keep doing what you know you should be doing. Everything will start to fall right in place in your life, and before you know it, your main focus will become to maintain and hold down strongly what has been given to you. The more you attain and have will be all worth it to keep haters out. You will not allow haters in to take, rob, steal, and bring you down, as well as to not allow haters to destroy that divine mother-and-daughter bond. Keep in mind always to know that haters waste their time very foolishly and have nothing better to do with their time but to show up and cause lots of havoc and turn good energies against one another if allowed to do so. You cannot let bad hate in; low negative energy get in your way. Remember love operates in positive, high self-esteem energy. Sometimes in life, the most alluring thing a mother and daughter can have is that alluring thing I like to call the confidence that shares. I am bold and positive that hate has to get back, step back, and sit down—if you know what I mean.

Mothers and daughters, don't be afraid to walk in an expressive way of letting others know that you have confidence, and of making a showing you know who you are and that you really do love yourself. It's all about who you are and being real bold sometimes at representing:

I love and do care 100 percent about my self-worth and am not giving in and caring about what those haters share and want to do. Remember, you don't have to let others bring you down to zero in your divine thinking. Do your best with using all your divine might, mothers and daughters, to take good care of yourself. Strive 100 percent to be happy. You know sad haters are out in the world; however, you keep being and doing what love represents, making things in your life go the good, prosperous way.

Always make it a positive habit to protect your mind from coming down to that level of how haters want you to come down to their level of blending in with their way of corrupt, twisted, confused, distorted thinking. Don't give in. It's best to keep blending in with a strong expression of love. That's all that matters—that's really what's of real importance. Remember love is all that really only cycles and makes the world really go round and round. Hate does not keep the cycle going round and round in our world. Hate just stops everything and kicks out poison and more poison.

Mothers and daughters, always remember you want love energy in your divine bond. Hate will do what it's best at really doing: bring you down, seriously destroy your energy and will to do what is of right performance. Hate will bring your energy down so low until you will become so weak as to moving around in a positive motion way. A mother and daughter really have to be real determined to keep hate from coming into their divine bond.

One way a mother and daughter can keep hate out is by keeping a connection with having positive goals and doing and using all their might at accomplishing what must be done and what has to be done in their near future. A lot of times, the only way haters get in and start making lots of effort at trying to break down that divine bond is when there is open space for that force to enter, and having goals makes a big difference in your life. And as mother and daughter, when you both are moving toward positive motion together at accomplishing and making things happen, no matter big goals or some goals could just be short-term goals, it does not really matter, goals or goals rather short term or long term. A simple goal really does matter and will make a big difference in a mother's life, as well as the same for the daughter's as well.

Haters will know that they just have to move on because of the divine art or practice of not allowing hate in to bring discomforting energy in to wretchedly destroy. Remember always, mothers and daughters of creation, you walk in divine love—not fear. The walk of fear stems and comes from that energy and motion of being afraid, of false evidence trying to appear and make itself of some sort and type of being real. Don't fall into this illusion. Now danger is real and does exist; however, staying in connection with your divine self, you will know danger from false fear. Danger is a real, proven force. Just always be, or become, more aware of not allowing those who are very miserable to come in and destroy that divine bond of love.

Remember, haters do hate what looks good, sounds good, and most certainly hate what's of good practice by nature. This is why it's so important for a mother and daughter to walk in nature together. Good practice of unity is so important, and always remember, don't let anyone with a bad heart and ill intent destroy what's given by the Divine Creator! Remember that those who hate lack the energy to practice the art of love. Remember, when you walk in love, you're guided the right way. When you walk in hate, your energy is really misguided. Those misguided live with so many problems and everybody else's problems as well. All this distorted behavior stems from a lack of self-control and from being very miserable.

I have always heard the saying that miserable ones enjoy bringing company into their confused, miserable lives if they are able to do so. This statement is very much true. Which is why you really must do your best at keeping haters far from and most certainly away from your divine bond that a mother and daughter does share from doing what's right around all angles of protecting themselves. Don't let anyone come into your life and cause extreme discomfort. Remember that people can only get away with what you allow; standing firm and meaning what you say and doing what you say let others know you stand on business, and you strictly mean business when it comes right down to doing and remaining firm with regards to your standards!

If you give and turn over all your rights of your own self-control, others will come in and take total control over you. This is why it's very important for a mother and daughter to bond very strongly and keep haters out. Never give haters control like that. Remember, haters don't care about you. That force only wants to bring you down so low and then find a serious way to step right on you and keep on in motion, as if nothing happened or occurred. That's the name of the game haters like to play.

Mothers and daughters of the world, remember you don't have to give in and accept and play this game of wicked control. Remember hate and haters have been around many, many years since the beginning of time; and the game of hate and wickedness have always been played on those who were open to it and too weak to keep it out. When its approach is staring you right in your divine face, mothers and daughters, you don't have to be, or become, weak to this old game played for many years and centuries. One strong reason as to why you don't have to be played from it and by it is it's more in the open now than ever.

The word *hate* is really well-defined and given so many definitions as to its meaning, not to mention so many young artists and rappers always rap and discuss who these real live haters are. Just stay and remain in the armor of love, and nothing can be done to you by these haters who operate in the force of darkness of bringing you down very low. Since the beginning of time, the rule has always been about good versus bad. Every day, just know what force to operate under, and keep that divine love connection at the center of your mother-daughter bond. Remember it's really okay to be and walk around happy. There's nothing crazy about being happy. It's great and so much fun every day to live a divine life. Staying connected to having a positive mother-and-daughter relationship is truly what it is all about.

Love is the most powerful gift you can give someone. The inner voice of love remember always just because of knowing how to think for yourself and listen to that inner voice, you only will become much more wise from it. Remember, haters sometimes will often think of smart thinkers as being crazy, and remember that divine ones don't believe and accept this fake statement. There are always some in the world who like to and get plenty of joy from hating on the Creator's chosen children. Remember it's all a low setup to get you to turn in on yourself. It's a wicked trap, which all you divine ones do not have to fall down into. Remember, the goal is to set out for achievement.

A mother and daughter really enjoy moving together and working together at maintaining and having and strive together in good motion. There is always lots and lots of strength you get from good motion; bad motion is just what you do not want to be a part of. Participation in good motion is what and only is of best intrance of taking part in, is where you want to go and be. Remember, in life, it's all about getting and attaining the positive results you so desire and want. Hate is truly not the result and solution for living a truly divine life and lifestyle. Remember the misguided ones are the wretched ones.

The youth's favorite word of their use is looking into someone's face, strong and stern, and really seeing if that person is wretched—which means miserable. Remember always that when someone is miserable, there is no caring at all about you and at the same time having no shame in their game at causing you to have extreme discomfort. However, the better you get at keeping haters out and away from your divine bond, you will start connecting and sharing energy with those who have a divine bond as well. Which is why, mothers and daughters, you must always do your best at protecting your bond that you share as mother and daughter, because the more you live life and understand life, you gain and start to see just why and how much of importance that bond really is not to be played with or ever taken for granted. Remember that a bond shared between a mother and daughter is really, really special and should and always be made on to others to see that it's of special closeness. Otherwise, others will do what some really know best—and that's to get in, destroy it, and bring high positive energy down to zero, just so you can think and operate from a low mind of thinking that will only get you nothing.

A mother and daughter must really know how to protect their hearts and do their best to anchor their hearts in love. Having the rhythm of a good heart will take you to many far, good places in your life, if you make a good and strong effort at protecting your heart. One of a lot of good ways of knowing the art of protecting your heart is to keep strong action at doing and moving around in a consistent and steady manner at doing and accomplishing all your important tasks. This is such a good way a mother and daughter can and will keep haters out and away from their divine bond. Darkness sometimes can be described in many ways. Like a tramp, it will keep coming back, and you just have to remain standing firm and tell the tramp to go away and stop coming back. And speak with authority;

use that force to let it be known that you're serious and not playing and that you mean business strictly and straight to the point.

Haters, go away, and know that your evil, distorted energy is not welcomed; and my divine love is not accepting and welcoming your energy of hate going nowhere. Hate energy is not welcome. It's wrong—a low, down energy that is really on its way out when right shows up. It just has to go leave. Get out, get away, and stay away! You almost have to have a BEWARE sign in your mind to say "keep out" and mean it.

Mothers and daughters of beautiful creation, remember the Creator gives us that divine choice. We can live in love and denounce hate. You just have to know and really understand your unique place in creation, our beautiful universe. Strive to keep the divine energy flowing well; let it flow like a beautiful waterfall. Use all your strength to see that your energy flows extremely well! Just don't play with hater energy. Don't welcome it, and it must flee. You really do have to be real committed from within to flow from love and keep hate out. Otherwise, you can and will become such an easy target for hate to come in and play your energy down. Just always remember that hate takes you nowhere and will only lead your thinking astray in the wrong lane, down a path of going nowhere toward self-destruction. Love will bring you right thinking and lots of joy. It's like walking in beautiful sunny, fresh air, listening to the beautiful sound of chirping from the birds. That's why it's just so good for a mother and daughter to do a lot of walking together. It helps protect that bond of realness that a mother and daughter have together.

Remember, haters don't know how to bond correctly and properly. What's only of knowing how to do as a hater is tear away tear at a divine bond. This is why it's so important that divine bonding is watched close and protected, just so you can see clearly and learn observation skills. Just so you can see if that wolf in sheep's clothing is really trying to get in and go at it to tear down a divine bond or set out to tear down your structure that is your protection around your divine bond. Remember that haters are very tricky and destructive, almost in contrast to the story of Little Red Riding Hood, how the wolf will huff and puff until the wolf can blow your house down if given a chance to do it, just because this is the energy of a seriously determined hater. If given the opportunity and chance at being able to do so, the Big Bad Wolf is like the hate and is going to do just that when thinking that its force can get in and destroy and tear down what was built up and around love—not by that force of hate, deceptiveness, and trickiness of bribes. These are all motions of bad rhythm and motives. You have to stand firm and stand up against it in right principles and not allow these wrong motions in to cripple you and break you down to zero.

There really does come a time in life you have to stand your ground regarding what you believe to be of right principles—and at the same time, don't back down. Because if you do, people will see this as a sign of weakness and come right in and go seriously at it to play you with a will so strong to make sure tearing you down is their number-one goal. Motion and rhythm like this are totally all wrong. Keep it out; don't let it in. This behavior gets you nowhere.

Remember, when you are going somewhere in life, you have to keep going somewhere. Eliminate/get rid of all time-wasting in your life and keep time wasters out of your divine life. You have to be elite. Choose to know a select group. And when I share an elite group, I am not talking about people who walk around with their noses stuck up in the air like they're better than human creation. However, what I am saying is you choose who you want to know and be around. You don't let others dictate and rotate their way into your divine life just because of others feeling as if it's their right to just come in and have access to you just because they want to. You have to live as if an iron fence were around your divine life.

A mother and daughter both have to practice this rhythm of motion; otherwise, people will be able to get in and break through your divine structure just so it can be shared that it was able to be done. Remember always how important it is for a mother and daughter to keep striving for perfection, and the only way to keep coming into strong perfection is by practice and staying in connection with right rhythm and right motion. This is what I like to call defense against hate and wrong motion. Remember you really do have to make a conscious effort at being and remaining alert skills to see what hate is and be very stern in all areas of your life, as to not allowing that negative force in because if let in, it's really going to try to break you down as well as the same break down your living structure also and for the power of real love that a mother and daughter operate in and live in.

Bad destructive behavior with bad motion will not be tolerated or allowed; foolishness is not permitted. Mother and daughter work together and build their life together like a strong pillar. All that hate does is self-destruct and tear down. You don't need this behavior and motion and really don't have time for it as well!

Always keep inside your mind what you need, and do not let in the wrong information that wants to program hate. Don't allow it in. Do not nourish hate or waste time promoting it, mothers and daughters. It gets you nowhere as well as takes you nowhere as well. You want to be able to stand strong and firm when haters try to pull your energy toward them and want you to go around them. You have to not participate in their circles of hate and confusion. That's all that it is, and it really just wants to keep you spinning and spinning around in a vortex of confusion. Stay away from it, and remember, you don't have to show up for what has no right benefit.

Keep in mind that haters could really care less about you receiving good rewards for your life and further into your future. All haters want to do is set your lifestyle up around theirs just to seek and find a way to bring your lifestyle up under subjection to their energy of hate. They just want to try to control you from flowing in love so hate can bring you down to zero. This is why it's so important to keep haters out and away from your divine bond. There is just no way you can ever trust a wolf anyway—or wolves, period. A wolf is going to seriously tear your house down if you let it in; and once inside, the wolf is going to keep coming back until it feels there is just nothing left to be torn down.

Mothers, you must be smart and think smart. Save your family legacy; it is your right to do so. Protect all your good inheritance and don't answer to a wolf in sheep's clothing when it tries to dial you up to participate with their flock! Remember you don't have to show up at the invite. Don't take nothing you don't want. The Creator gives us all free will to pick and choose. We all have choices, so this is why it's better to know how to make the best choices for our lives. When you make good, sound logical choices for your life, it makes situations have more of a smooth and easy right turnout!

Mothers and daughters, you have to use all your senses' sound, high mental capacity. Always keep in mind that others will not share with you most of the time what they're really up to and what their original plan is to get in and break that divine bond. You have to be on point guard so when given a strong chance at will to see what's really going on, you will have strong willpower to strike back. However, if you're not using your senses the way you really should, you are going to be taken down and taken advantage of by others just because of not being keen having mental alertness. You have to retain in one's good possession at all times, knowing how to be kept in your own divine fortress.

When a mother and daughter live by these divine rules, you most certainly will be able to keep those with that wolf-dog like predatory mammals away others wolfish deceptive behavior really won't have a way of affecting you, as well as infecting you. Using your senses will teach you, at all times, how to really protect yourself and keep that fence of protection around yourself and your aura, which is so much needed in these trying times of the world we live in today.

A mother and daughter must always keep developing their beautiful brains. It is just a must. There is just no way around from keeping a way from doing so. A mother must be a very good, strong example as to why fear and blockage energy must not get in the way of creativity and creative energy. Taking full ownership over your life is what I like to call true, real freedom! Remember, mothers and daughters, every possibility is open to you for constant development of all your beautiful creativity. There are just no limitations; keep at it and embrace your life. Stay connected to the creative essence of your life; allow the Creator to remain at the central core of your life, as well as staying connected to creation. This rhythm, most definitely, will run haters away. Hate can't move through the real divine power of love; it just can't do so! All the love force asks of you and requires of you to do is just to turn your love energy up high. Use your love high beams, and hate has to bow to love and get on. Don't let fear get in your way.

Mothers and daughters, keep fear out, far away from you, and watch and see how it will be much of an easy task for you to really create. You will start to bring into being of a reality so many different wonderful ideas. You will be able to keep at it and keep at it. I just have to remind you to always give, and don't forget to give credit to the Almighty, the Creator who gives us our divine gifts. It is our divine gifts that keep us happy and bring more happiness into our beautiful lives. As mothers and daughters, we just have to learn and keep practicing the divine art of embracing our gifts in the clasp of open arms so we can receive plenty of room to share our gifts through the art and power of love.

It is very important that we listen to our divine inner self and follow our inner revolution. This will only help and assist in carrying out an outer revolution in our lives. A mother and daughter must essentially practice the art from all aspects in their lives to face all shadow aspects of self! Staying connected to the divine self will most certainly keep haters out and away from your divine self, as well as help you stay connected to your divine gifts. It is always good and very helpful to have good insight and to look around at your surroundings with clear thinking. This will allow you to smell the scent of love in the air when you're around carrying positive energy, just as well. Hate brings on a foul low-energy vibration, which will only make you want to keep on trucking by it—not stop to entertain it or participate in any hate language.

These are the rhythms and motions that a mother and daughter must keep developing in order to keep hate rhythm and hate motion out. Otherwise, the rhythm of hate and the language of hate will dominate its way in and all around your life and divine lifestyle. Remember, a wolf doesn't care; it just wants to eat its prey if it can be done and seriously gotten away with. It is for this reason alone that a mother and daughter must seriously—in a strong, strong manner—be a strong, supportive team for each other, using their minds' will not to come up under others' minds and will of subjection to do wrong and fall down mentally for weak prey from others! This is why it's so important to stay and remain connected to your inner self.

Find all your inner gifts, mothers and daughters. Find all your hidden gifts inside yourself, and really do your best to embrace them, knowing your gifts will aid you so well in having power to use your gifts to enjoy your everyday lifestyle. Then practice the art of exercising the strong use of your gifts. There is that saying that practice really does make you better at accomplishing any thing. You really will not want haters around at all, just because you don't have time for that low energy of a vibration frequency. Your inner gifts operate from a very high place at a very high vibration from within yourself, so that's why sometimes, the spirit of low procrastination will try to enter to stop you from your higher climb into yourself. This is why it's just so important to keep hate out, because you want to keep that high climb upward in and toward your gifts just to reap the outside rewards of bringing good manifestation to your life in the way you want your life to evolve and be every day.

Mothers and daughters, protect and take your divine life and lifestyle very seriously. Remember, we all only get one life on divine earth, and we really must do our best to guard it with divine protection, as well as enjoy our lives. Remember we live in a world where darkness and hate does exist. Darkness and hate energy are very real. These forces can and will try to bring our actual being of ourselves down if we are weak to not having awareness of these forces and allow these low-energy drains in. It's important that as strong human beings on earth, our existence is of being outstanding and having lots of courage, having that ability to conquer fear or despair. There is just no way that hate can really win when a mother and daughter have strong, powerful deliberations of togetherness. Keep abhorrent hate energy away and know when and where you are and who you are around to not allow or produce bad motion on yourself!

Writing on this strong subject really does require a lot of words to be repeated over and over, and all that is to say that sometimes, hearing or reading something once is really not enough. It needs to be heard, or said, more than one time. In all of my sayings as I end this chapter, my exit of conclusion, I hope I have been able to share in the deep realms and worlds for all my beautiful readers. Mothers and daughters, walk in love, live in love, and all else of good showing are sure to come about.

The Protection of
Mother-Daughter Bond

From the very minute, the very second, the moment my beautiful daughter Ameerah Naajidah Bilil laid on my heart after giving beautiful birth of coming into this world called earth, I didn't for one second guess what my real job would be for her! Protect! Protection. I didn't get caught up in those superficial jobs that a high, strong percentage of society try and tell a mother what's best for her and what she must, and should, do for her child. My heart clearly shared with me: "Don't worry about food, shelter, and clothing. Your most and first concern is and should be that you protect this beautiful life that the Creator has given you to protect at this very moment! And all else will be taken care of—you just protect this child and keep living with faith and by faith."

One of my favorite scriptures is "The just shall live by faith. Now faith is the substance of things hoped for, the evidence of things not seen." When a mother truly learns the real art of protecting her daughter—or in some situations, her daughters—everything else falls right in line. A real, true mom knows how important real safety really is for her daughter; so therefore, a mom is going to put safety around her offspring. Trust me, I do understand how clothing, food, and shelter are very much so as important, and how everyone must and has to eat as well. And we all need somewhere to live and stay as well! However, in a lot of cases from myself doing research, some mothers will rush right back out into the workforce before really doing research as to what environment their newborn baby will lay their head on until the return of the mother. Mothers that allow this kind of situation to take place are lacking protection skills! When a child cannot even talk and tell what's going on around them, this is not a good way for a mom to start out. I know you need money. You need your job so you can eat and take care of your offspring. However, what you must seriously think about is that you should know what really comes first while you are out in the world working: is safety around that child?

Safety and protection around a mother-daughter bond starts the minute that child comes out of the womb. In order to do right and well and focus right on your work in the workforce, a good mother has to know from within that she has done her real job first, made sure so much safety is in and around where her baby is left—in most situations, at least eight to nine hours. Otherwise, she knows she will spend those total nine hours going seriously crazy, worrying about her baby girl if she is a mother who cares. This is the first stage of protection that a real mother will do; she knows she must seriously provide that safety.

Keep in mind, a newborn baby girl is not a toy or a little doll—something that you move around and play with, stop and put it down when you're finished or tired. A baby girl is a brand-new life, which means from the time of being birthed into the world, there goes some serious responsibility, all the way until she reaches womanhood and adulthood. Me, personally, I do not see how a responsible mother could let others have access to taking their young baby infant around to go to other houses, and your baby cannot even talk or speak about her surroundings, as well as for the worst. If someone does something wrong, the infant cannot even inform anyone. So if my baby girl cannot talk, you are not going to show her off like some sort of showpiece, as the young ones like to quote. It is just not going down!

I have witnessed this lack of protection and safety in the inner cities—most of the time, from real young mothers. It's very sad, but it is also the truth. I would like to go further into speaking on the word *responsibility* or *responsible*. Definition: "answerable for acts or decisions, able to fulfill obligations, having important duties." I will make it plain and simple. Being a mother is a very important duty, or a task that is performed with high skill in and all the time! I know in modern society, as myself speaking right now, the energy about being a mother is sometimes made for women to fall into thinking that motherhood is not as important as being a nurse, a schoolteacher, a doctor or attorney, or some other high-name title. However, if you break each and every word down to its true meaning, a mother takes on each and every title I just mentioned when she performs her duty and role of being that powerful mother. I am here to say to all you powerful mothers out in the world: know your role and learn it with skills, and add and bring more skills to yourself as being a mother, and watch and see how so many greatly rewarding blessings are really waiting to be given to you! It's really time to sound that alarm as to who and how great mothers really are. Always remember and know why the protection of a mother-and-daughter bond is just so extremely of value and importance.

I had to just give you a brief description about infant stage of protection. Now I will get into more of the protection of the mother-daughter bond on an everyday basis and out through a mother's and daughter's lives. Protection starts the minute a mother or daughter wakes up in the morning and hits the streets—rather, it is because of one or the other going to work or school or, in some cases, just to decide to take a long faith walk or just to leave your home environment for fun and adventure. Beware, my mothers and daughters, the wolves are there, ready to see how to seek at you to pull your positive-energy force field to zero, their low vibration. The way you sound your inner alarm within yourself turns your inner vibration up real high at staying focused at doing what is right; and that is staying on your individual, single journey at doing good every day. And this positive motion will keep taking you and stirring your life in a right positive direction.

A mother and daughter must walk in a protection realm of right. This will only help in all areas of life at doing and accomplishing what should be sought after. Unity is very important, but it's only just a word if not really practiced. A mother and daughter must be very aware of that silent inner power; being able to hear their inner voice is a protector in its own self just because so many humans today in the world don't really care enough about themselves to silence their beings just so hearing of what's taking place within themselves as well as to what they're around! I like to call this your inner divine protection, taking the time to slow your inner pace down and just plain listen when you tap into your listening psyche, your soul and mind. You come to find a lot of deep, hidden answers to all your challenging situations of dispute. This will not only bring protection around your mother-and-daughter bond, this will also bring more protection around a mother and daughter all throughout life just because you will be able to, in such a strong and dedicated way, seek out inner answers to different trying situations that can sometimes surface into one's life!

Another divine way I have learned throughout living is another way of protection that a mother brings around her daughter—certain things and certain places a mother may go and attend. It does not necessarily mean that these places are of such a welcome for your daughter. I am not saying that when a mother goes in and out of different places or environments, you keep your daughter away and out from them because it's bad and dangerous. Know that's not what I am sharing. My point is some things that a mother does and some places a mother goes to is just for yourself. We all have our own karma and our own divine journey, which will lead us further into ourselves and what's best for our own lives. It's just not a wise suggestion. Keep your daughters out of—what I like to call them— your own twists and turns that you may have had to take in your life in order to become the great woman that you are.

As women, whether we like to admit it or not, sometimes we do experience, participate, and live certain situations—and/or have been places that are just not and were not always in our best interest and outcome for our lives, and most certainly not for us to bring in and expose our daughters to. I am not sharing this to oppose or face confrontation with my readers. I am sharing this so you can become aware of your own entanglements and so you can make a strong effort not to allow yourself to bring your daughter into your entanglements. I have seen so many mothers do just what I have just mentioned! And guess what, you are slipping. Your daughter now is just sitting around at someone else's house that you would always visit; however, this place, this household environment, has nothing to do with your daughter.

All I am sharing is watch out for this motion. It really could get your daughter caught up. This is not her path. You are supposed to be helping your daughter come into herself and helping to guide her on her right divine path for her life. This is what mother-and-daughter protection is all about. So, as mothers, we must answer up to what our duties are. Forget the haters and naysayers, we have to do our real job, and that starts with protection—keeping that bond of protection around your daughter! Keep in mind, when you have a good bond with your daughter, a good and positive moving-further relationship, others will try to practice manipulation and the power of influence over a strong mother-and-daughter relationship if really given a chance, especially if their thinking is based around being able to get away with their deceitful behavior of deception. Sometimes you do have to sound off your mental alarm, letting it be well known that you are so much very aware what you see is taking place and that you're not with allowing wrong, deceptive behavior in your life to take you down or play yourself and your daughter back down in a downhill spiral of their own confusion.

Stay watchful, mothers and daughters, and always remember your divine help and protection will always come in from the Creator. Just stay very aware! I know sometimes there is that percentage of people that you may cross paths with; and before you know it, they're doing all that can be done to get in your space to try to control it. And at the same time, they will try to take over your mind and tell you what you should do, as well as your daughter at the same time.

Remember, mothers and daughters, we are leaders for our own lives that were given to us by the Creator, not those naysayers. We have to protect ourselves every morning by getting up and doing what the Creator tells us to do, and where to show up and go. This behavior is protection in itself. I like to call it self-control. When you don't have self–control, you start to fall for anything; and sometimes what others want to offer you is not always best for you, beautiful mothers and daughters. Even though it works for others and that's what is of enjoyment for them—remember that's them, not you.

Remember to stay in and around your band of protection, mothers. Remember always it is a must that you learn and always practice the real and true art of knowing, learning, and accepting the true facts that you do really have to take good care of your own self. As mothers, you're that great example for your daughters in the home, as well as for daughters whom we pass by from time to time that look upon us as of viewing and seeing how things are done from us.

Whenever a mother and daughter do things in the art of togetherness and from a united stance, others will always watch. It's perfectly okay. This just means that you're just doing something right. This is why knowing how to focus is so important. It will keep others out of your way in life. Sometimes, others will make it their business to get in your business if they think and believe it could be gotten away with. However, when that mother-and-daughter bond is well tied and linked in strong unity, what's of value and is of strength can sometimes shake the weak up in a real way.

Sometimes in life, there does come about a time when you will have to confront the weak, the negative, to keep it pushing. Otherwise, it will try to take over your life. A real mother is going to always inform her daughter of all the games and tricks that will be tried to win her over. This is why having committed goals are good; it helps you see yourself meet your own finish line. And for the most part, you do not want to disappoint yourself, not to mention how happy you really are when you accomplish what you set your mind out to attain. There's so much divine protection arriving at the finish line in life. You will become like a bow and arrow for your life most of the time. There's that saying, "If you're not for me, then you must be against me." So therefore get back, stay out of my way in a real, for sure way.

Being truthful is another form of protection for a mother-daughter bond. When you practice this art of being truthful with each other, your radar will really become better at keeping falsehood out. Remember, so many want light in their lives; however, so many really do fall when it's of showing respect for light or doing right by energy of light. And that's from getting comfortable in darkness and, of course, from being lazy!

Let's talk about being pure lazy. This is a rhythm, a motion, that a mother must never fall down in, and not to mention never allow the energy of laziness to overtake her daughter. When one is lazy, it is a disliking feeling of exertion. Now there is a difference of being in a sleepy state and wanting and needing rest. The feeling of getting and needing rest is a natural suspension of consciousness, which is okay. Now that energy of being and feeling lazy is a low energy that causes you to feel drained, and it also will draw you to drain others of their energy. The person that is lazy cover will be pulled easy by the person who is not lazy; however, a person who is not lazy will not let you get away with doing this to them. Remember, high energy people know that real rest is really needed in order to be themselves as well as enjoy themselves, which is why when a mother and daughter keep that bond of protection around them, both will be able not to fall down in lazy energy.

There are all different kinds of ways lazy energy can be explained. Have you ever been around someone who is always complaining? This or that something is just always wrong. That person suffers from being purely lazy. So this is why if you keep engaging in a conversation with them, or you stay around them too long, you will start feeling drained as if you are lazy too.

There is protection in knowing how to stop wrong, bad motion because if you don't, it is going to just drag at you and really pull you down. Sometimes you just have to say enough is just enough. Mothers and daughters, take control over your beautiful lives. Being lazy really does not get you anywhere you want to go and arrive at the finish line in your life, and when you're lazy, you will not even show up at the finish line. Remember, mothers and daughters, you only get one life—so live it to your best ability. Don't allow others to come in and rob and try to take your joy!

Trust me for one second if thought of being able to do so that is what will be done! You have to think and operate in a mind-set of protection and always be aware so that you don't entertain lazy energy. You want to keep your energy very upright and very focused in all areas of your life so you can get what needs to be done by and from you. Mothers and daughters, you must have developed energy that moves and rotates in a structed aim way this is and the only way of facing what's of a stare right in front of you sometime that mirror of what needs to be accomplished and what's need it from us mothers and daughters going into are near further can and sometimes is very painful.

However, taking your path in a warrior's way and stance can and will make a lot of situations and tasks a much more easy road for daily success and accomplishment. Remember there are those out there in the world who will seriously do their best to get in and around just to see if that divine protection that a mother and daughter have—just to see if it can be broken down in an easily distorted way.

What I recommend for the mother-daughter bond is to stick with your original plan and get up and go do what you both think is of best entrance for your lives. Take pleasure in being happy for that divine protection. It is all around you. When you set your heart out to do and accomplish what you know has to be done, no given excuse is approved and allowed entry.

Another golden way a mother and daughter can protect themselves is by being themselves. It is great to be yourself. Don't worry about being different. You are different, and it is perfectly okay. Being yourself does give you a divine protection around your aura. You will stand out from the crowd. Remember, self does carry heavy weight sometimes. A lot of times, others look you on and just watch just because of their not really being their selves. Mothers and daughters, keep your protection aura around your being; you will feel so good about being who you are. The more grounded a mother and daughter are, there will be much better and good outcomes of manifestation in and around all areas of your life. A lot of times when a mother and daughter set out to take care of their own business and go do and accomplish what's of importance and sometimes what's of fun as well. This not only gives you the skill of staying focused, it protects you as well. It is the power of protection of doing what you say you're going to do.

When mothers and daughters do their best to keep busy, it really does keep you out of getting in trouble with others. Remember, we are all responsible for our own divine life force—no one else. So this is why it's just so very good for a mother to set a good example for her daughter. A good living example equals protection. Doing good and living well will always lead and direct your life and lifestyle into positive situations and positive results. Remember, divine protection is like playing a game of chess. A mother and daughter have to have real close range at how to stay and remain in the protective realm in and all around their lives. There are always thoughts and situations of others that want you to come out of your protective realm so you can turn yourself into their pawn of their joy of having and owning control of sacrifice over you. This is why a mother and daughter have to think as in a way like playing chess at all times in their lives, not letting others take you out and away from your own mental realm of protection.

Remember that people will try to get in to challenge you, or dispute, making all efforts at competing with you, wanting you, mothers and daughters, to get from up under your protective umbrella. Sometimes you must fight hard from within to not allow others with their strong, twisted, distorted will to swing at trying to do as what I just mentioned. Remember, the protection of a mother-daughter bond has always been of real strength and will stay as real as the strength of iron. The more we are made aware of this divine-given strength, it will help others to see it and, at the same time, come to terms with how powerful and real it is. Real is always being genuine the same the real true fact as of appearance being self and living for yourself, not living for others and worrying what others think and not caring what negative people have to say and communicate about you. Keeping your thinking right and protected as well. You want to always remain in real control of your thinking and thought process as well anyway!

A mother and daughter is a strong team together, ready to always make an extra-strong effort at winning in all areas of their lives. Being a winner is also another form of protecting yourself. It's always a great reward when we win in and at life situations. All this leads to different forms of protection. A mother and daughter must keep their mental wavelength connected from a mental wavelength of protection when you think right and really pay attention to your mental waves of what to do and how to take care of what needs to be done. Protection for and around your mother-and-daughter bond starts becoming just a way of life. You both start being more convinced of your automatic protection system from within.

A real, true mother wants a positive protective environment for her daughter, and it starts from within and from mental protection. When you think protection, you also start to live protection and walk protection—not living in fear but, most certainly, being and becoming very extra aware of your area and your surroundings. One of the reasons most people walk around from an energy of fear is because their thought process is very scattered. Scattered thinking really can and does bring on bad energy and will cause troubled energy that takes you from your mental umbrella of protection. So one of the first laws of protection is self—you protecting your mind, knowing how to tell your own self to keep away and stay away from wrongdoing and wrong actions. It's a lot of teamwork that a mother and daughter practice together—throwing the baton, making sure the baton is caught before it falls down to the ground.

There is power between the protection of a mother and daughter. A mother is really going to use all her power and might to make sure protection is around her daughter. Just in case she does fall down, a real mom is and will show her daughter how to swing and get back up! In and throughout life, we are all subject to make some mistakes. When you learn from a mistake, it causes you to view a mistake from close-up range. You can grow from mistakes and most certainly learn from them; however, when a mother and daughter follow a guide or live by a guideline of protection for their own lives, it will add and put more and keep divine protection around their mother-and-daughter bond.

There are so many mothers and daughters in the world today who really do not have a serious guide for their everyday lives, and as a result, so many snares and hooks and baits await for a mother and daughter to fall into. Remember, good behavior has a plan for your life; and bad has a plan as well. This is why when a mother and daughter use both their senses together, it adds more protection. Knowing and using your senses in a very well-controlled way will and can help you see things and situations for your life in a very right way of motion simply because there are just so many people in the world who really enjoy manipulating, trying to influence and gain cunning behavior over someone's life if they think that you're not using your senses at your highest ability. This is why knowing and understanding how your senses work is another rule of protection around a mother-and-daughter bond!

A mother must teach her daughter how to stay connected to how her brain operates in right motion and not come up under the control of others. When a daughter remains teachable, a real and true mother has so much powerful insight that can really help her daughter. This only allows the protection of their bond to become much stronger at becoming and doing what's right for their lives. The protection of a mother and daughter consists of being of inherently strong and unique counsel. This is a must—an art that must be practiced very accurately with the power of a mother and daughter bond.

Another powerful form of protection, a mother and daughter must also know their form of their own language of communication of protection. Sometimes you just don't want to communicate with others in their language of disrespect, not going anywhere. So therefore, when a mother and daughter decide to communicate in their proper way of understanding what's of sharing of them, this will keep that force of while crazed, wrong, uncontrolled bad energy completely out no real, strong, smart mother and daughter have any time for this foolish, going-nowhere, distorted energy. Whether it's accepted or not, it's about business every single moment. There is always something that needs to be done, a call to be made, something of a serious matter—a serious subject matter to be taken care of. This is just how it is. Yes, being tough is not an option. It is just a rhythm: a motion that just has to be produced.

As you see and clearly understand, a real mom-and-daughter bond of protection cannot be played with and most certainly cannot be taken for granted. People tend to have right out no respect for anyone who can be easily walked on, stepped on, or in many ways, who allow themselves to be taken advantage of seriously by others— which is why protection starts just from you yourself as a mother standing firm and, most certainly, grounded in her morals and conduct of protective behavior from just knowing how she should think! As a positive result, a daughter will example her mom, stance however, in some golden way, maybe much stronger and firmer just because of being well taught from her mom.

A mother rewarding examples of good conduct is watched by her daughter, who is very intelligent and smart. She will watch and pay close attention as to how she practices the real art called using your smarts, carrying it out in a common-sense, high mental capacity and using your brain in a very sound way. Why is real protection at its highest their is so of much arguments fights of disturbance that can really be done away with if the mind is used in high realm and good thinking. I like to call it common sense. When your common-sense senses are really being used, you—as a mother—become very seeing, making sure deeds and important talks are really being performed.

A real mom does understand why meeting with an escort is really of importance for her daughter. It just seems that when others know that there is someone around watching and caring to watch at that evil eye that others have at times and try to hide. A good escort of smarts can really recognize what another person reality is being conducting itself as. Self-righteousness is really just being convinced of one's own choices of righteousness, which is why a mother and daughter's right thinking brings into play right motion of seriousness for real protection. You have to get up and give right action a serious for real way of life there are times that in your way of lifestyle things tasks and different situations and difficult tasks will come as challenge for a mother and daughter for certain these difficult tasks is what keeps their protection around their bond. This is why no matter how hard it can get and how tough it may become for a mom and daughter, both must keep at it every day to succeed in their beautiful lives and get where they are going. Being obedient to where you're going, and what is expected and of what must be done is only and will produce the kind of results and rewards you must have for your life.

Another rule that applies to and for protection of and for a mother-and-daughter bond is never take you yourself—your life and time—for granted. Not taking your life for granted alone will protect you just because you will for most certainly know you really don't have any and no time to waste. When time is wasted, you're not up under the power of protection. It's just better for a mother and daughter to have and practice unity of their time being of importance and of value just so mom and daughter can really get to the places and things of where the places and things must be done and sought after. Time is really more precious than most people give it consideration. Most people don't take notice at all; there is no observing close attention to how you cannot at all get back any time you send forth or use. So why waste it?

There is so much protection for a mother and daughter if just taken of giving a second in how their time is valued and spent, especially when there is just so much in particularly or notably that can and must be done. A second does go by fast; however, you still must keep this in mind eternity infinite duration is somewhere in that second, which is why a mother and daughter have no time to waste at all. When others think that a mother and daughter don't value their time and feel as if there are ways and situations of allowing their energy and force field to pull you down into doing and wasting your time—guess what? That's exactly what will be done.

So therefore, mothers and daughters, be straight up straightforward. Let others know exactly where you're coming from. To explain this in a much more clear explanation, be real. Demonstrate a conversation in quick motion and rhythm. *Don't waste my time; I am not going to waste your time.* However, get to the point. Remember, mothers and daughters, I truly do believe people only will and can get away with what you let them get away with. Stop caring about people who mean you no good—stand firm, stay grounded, and punch back (if you know what I mean). This will only make life more of ease and enjoyment. The protection of your mother-daughter bond will now be just as hard as a rock. You get what I am saying. You got it, so now just hold on to this truth.

The Rules of Space between
a Mother and Daughter

I s space really mandatory between a mother and daughter? I thought you knew! Yes, everyone needs it and must keep space the distance in their lives in order to keep peace, as well as remain peaceful. This is a very important rule in the home for a mother and daughter: even though we reside together, space is a must, not a choice.

Let me explain or give you the definition of *space*. It is a "period of time: area in around, or between: region beyond earth's atmosphere." The definition of space explains the word *space* in itself. A mother and daughter both will always come to a point in time where being separated is nothing and only but something good. As I write, of course I am thinking as well how it is very sad how so many grown women—supposedly according to what their age is—are really just still children when it comes to them either being in their homes alone being of so much codependent on their husband's energy as well at the same time, with any and everyone who is in their presence home at the time.

Everyone needs space. You would expect this to be common behavior; however, I am starting to really believe it does start from the space given between a bond with mother reason of saying this is their really is nothing too much of more stronger and strength besides that powerful beautiful bond with a mother, however space is still needed and of a required rule. When a mother and daughter give each other space, it shows and gives off such a high regard of respect. Having respect is not only showing good character between a mother and daughter; it also teaches you to have respect for others and, at the same time, respect their space as well. When you leave your home and go out into the world of life—what I call daily living—there is just so much space invasion from supposed individuals who call themselves grown adults. However, a high percentage can be sat down of question. Just because there is no respect of giving and refraining themselves from being in someone's space! You almost have to question: where did this mannerism of ill behavior come from? Is it from not being taught space in the home?

Yes, I really do believe that most of this behavior really does start from within our homes, which is why information must be given with regards as to why there must be real space between a mother and daughter in the home. How many of my beautiful readers can relate to all those so-called friendships with others who may be real friends or who just show intent of friendship but, however, start trying to get extra close up or in a close range of where of shouldn't be but, however or for some strange reason don't care but will still enter more close up on your space. You know what this is called: straight-up disrespect of your own right, your own space. Case in point, period! Stop them; don't allow it. Fight back with a mental punch from within. Tell them. Let it be known. Get back, or in some cases, get the hell back! You know, let's just keep it 100 percent real. You are in my space/zone, and guess what. No, I don't like it right now, and I never will. So just kick rocks and stop it right now.

When you feel like you are about to get into a confrontation with someone, or you notice that the other person is trying to push your mental buttons where you're not in control and the other is trying for you and wanting you to give them all your mental strength, just back them up. This means that they're trying to get further close up, and permission was not given to them. Tell them to back up: you're getting too close, too near in my space/zone. When you recognize this behavior, you start to immediately feel drained, which only leads to extreme mental distress, pain of agony of the mind. Remember, it's not you—it's the other person trying to inflict their mental poison on you, and they're doing it because of wanting control over you and your space. Keep them back; don't allow it. Sometimes it could be good to ask, "Did your mother give you space in the home while you were growing up?" Don't be surprised if you see their eyes turn red and someone really getting thrown off their weak game of trying to invade someone's space! The truth can hurt.

What I have learned from being around different types of people is that most of them really do not want to be exposed for what they're doing, or what they're trying to get away with. Oh well, do it anyway. It's about taking care of yourselves, mothers and daughters; and the best way of doing it is to seriously be and become more honest with and within self. One thing's for sure, a mother and daughter must know their space is a must and keep that space as well. Mothers and daughters, it is very important to remain at staying very dedicated in regards to what your beliefs are; otherwise, people will pull on your energy and rhythm like a serious game of tug-of-war. Don't let them claim your space for your life; remain grounded in good rules.

Let's talk about some of the rules that will take place in the boundaries with a strong mother and a well-trained, dedicated daughter. Rule number 1: do you respect each other's thoughts and thinking space? The reason I ask this serious question is because this is where it all starts from in regards to respecting each other's space, as well as to how you create inside the home and what and how you will produce what you want your reality to be. It is very important to let each other finish with your words of communication.

I have seen so many mothers throughout my life always screaming loudly at their daughter, or daughters, like madwomen gone crazy, totally out of their minds. This is not a good behavior to let your daughter see in the home or residence. All this does and will do is teach your daughter that she can and must scream and lash back out at you. This behavior is definitely not good. If this kind of behavior goes on inside the house, the respect of space for a mother and daughter is definitely not present!

In the home, so much really does start with our thoughts. A mother and daughter must communicate with each other in a peaceful, serenely tranquil way. It can be done; however, screaming and hollering are not severe and tranquil a lot of screaming and hollering just cause is a zero of understanding. As mothers, you can get your point across well and understood from tranquil language. Try it; you will be amazed. Now remember, practice does bring in much better results. People respond as to how they're used to of treatment is, so why not mothers and daughters. Let's make it a good habit of respecting each other's space; only good can be the center of having rules of space.

It's okay for a daughter to have firm boundaries. Most likely, if a daughter sees that her mother is firm and sharp in regard to what she stands for, a daughter will be strict as well in other areas. A lot of her boundaries will start with her room. She will create her room and space according to how she likes it. A viberate daughter knows that her room is really her private space and not, in any way, to do or practice wrong behavior in her room. However, she will want the design of her room from her will of creation. For example, as a mother, you may want to purchase a canopy bedroom set, whereas your daughter may voice her opinion at that moment and share that she wants a day bed. That's perfectly okay; let her have that day bed for her room. The point I am making is that the daughter knows it's her room because she is the one who will sleep in there. So therefore, let her be comfortable in choosing what bed will bring comfort and keep a smile on her face at the same time.

There is nothing wrong for a daughter to practice the art of making decisions. Yes, as mothers, there are times when we have to step back and let our daughter make choices about certain situations and matters. It is also okay to allow our daughter that space to think and create on the computer as well. Yes, it's okay to peek in and monitor at some distance; and from that point, we must allow our daughter, or daughters, to have at what should be done and completed by them in time of space. It is very important to request space when you live among others in your home, and if you find it just so difficult to complete paperwork, or you just can't create an environment to start reading a good book as well as finish your reading, this could mean there are no rules or any strict guidelines as to a space environment, and of giving others their space of a primitive of relating to characteristic of an early stage of a mother's development with her daughter at of young age given.

If respect of space is present, a mother and daughter will have no problems in this area of giving each other due respect, all due to having guidelines of respect set at an early stage in their living environment. Teaching in a home is of so much of requirement from a mom for her daughter the proper setting of space perfect example: When a mom is in the kitchen and she sets out to start teaching her daughter how to prepare food and make fun stuff like chocolate chip cookies, there first must be an environment of respect so the student of learning should not feel dumb just for not knowing. You are not dumb; you are just in the process of learning. Therefore, the teacher—the mom—must provide an environment of questions to be asked in the space of teaching.

Some mothers and daughters have a very hard and difficult time bringing unity in the kitchen, which I personally see this rhythm of motion not as a good one of practice for the art of unity with a mom and daughter. Just because a mother-and-daughter bond is of very much power and is very pleasant and there is much reward for a mother and daughter to prepare well good delicious very pleasing for the stomach good food and the smell of good aroma all and throughout the kitchen passing throughout other areas in the home from mother and daughter in the kitchen preparing wholesome great food, everything in the kitchen is spaced out right, so therefore, the food is excellent.

Remember, it's always okay to leave room for learning and an environment for space. The foundation for teaching is a must. When living in a structured environment, a mother and daughter must always come together to think and plan great events and great fun and rewarding situations for themselves, and the same for their lifestyle as well.

It is very rewarding for a mom and daughter to have greatness to look forward to. By sharing respect for space when inside the home, a mom and daughter will know how to give each other space when doing and conducting and taking care of important business. When outside the home sometimes, when I am out shopping or getting groceries, I see so many people in general and lots of mothers and daughters smothering each other—just no respect for space for one another, deprived of thinking space as well as breathing space. This is not a good rhythm for anyone to be in and, most certainly, not for a mother and daughter. We all need that extra fresh air of breathing space.

Being a grown adult, what I have given notice about demanding space on having no fear at keeping others where the belonging is supposed to be, it keeps you in a living environment of seeing and knowing and how to do what's best for yourself and your own life and lifestyle. So many individuals over the age of eighteen still get and remain so entangled with other people's lifestyles. Some just walk right into someone else's space, especially when thinking someone is successful and if you're trying to see if and that you can and may be able to get something of what you think they're having or owning. This is all wrong behavior. It's almost like thinking you have an access pass where, in reality, the other no-access pass was given to you to place in your hand. So then you go just jumping in someone else's space.

A mother must begin to teach her daughter strong values of having rules of success. First of all, people who have success in their lives, and have hard and concrete goals, are already used to people either always saying something to them as well as always trying to get in their space. So therefore, keeping armor for protection is what they already know how to do best anyway. So therefore, you are really wasting your own time trying to get in extra close.

Goals are very powerful to have. Just because it gives you no time to have to waste, so therefore, space distracters stop trying to evade others' space. It only shows that you're of an immature nature, which is defined as "you're a grown adult, but from within, you inflict childish behavior on to others." This is not a good behavior pattern to set.

Invading space and introduction are not the same. There is a way to introduce yourself and not come off as rude. However, rushing in and rushing up on someone in a disrespectful way is not a good thing or a good behavior. It only shows that you are not giving respect, and that you are at you own mercy as well as at the mercy of another for being very disrespectful. And at the same time, you are being viewed as someone who is very desperate, a projection of being extremely intense on to someone else. This is so not good. It's not going to really get you anywhere extra; and if you're not extra careful, it can and will lead you directly to the nuthouse. Or if not there you will live as a person who is infested with lots of serious problems and issues. And guess what, those who get up every day and think and plan do not want you around. So just grow up.

So, mothers and daughters, it starts a lot with us. We have to really practice every day at keeping it just so simple and give each other respect and space. Then you will be so able to maintain a clear perception when leaving your home. Remember, the name of this game is life; keep that space so you can keep seeing and knowing what your movements are and what they should be. When a mother and daughter practice the art of space, it only adds more preparation for keeping that crab-crab pulldown energy off you, and of knowing how to keep it at a distance and at bay from doing research and facts on of the main reasons for so much confrontation between a percentage of mothers and daughters. It is over crowding each other's space. Everyone needs their space.

In some cases, I have witnessed, seeing how others have gotten extremely upset just because of strong boundaries being set—that it would not be tolerated, allowing others the golden access pass to enter in and bring that dirty confusion in and around one's space. There is nothing wrong with that rhythm of "back it on up sometime." You must really let it be known that you demand space; otherwise, people will show up all in and around that divine space a mother and daughter have. Some will even go as far as shoving and pushing their way in and around that space.

Another rule of space a mother will give her daughter is she will allow her daughter that space to go in the kitchen sometimes to cook, as well as make tea or desserts, without any interruptions. In a household where there are just so many interruptions between a mother and daughter, it is just not a good behavior of fashion to practice, which only results to why timing is and of so much importance. Paying attention to time and small details means that awareness is taking place. Strong, keen awareness will block out unwanted distractions of interruptions, which is why a mother knows that if she practices self–control, it can and will only lead her daughter to have self-control. And that means not even allowing calls of distractions of interruption to come through and get next to your space when space is a requirement in the home.

You will also know, when you're at home, how to keep space even from incoming calls. I mean I know at lot of people talk a lot on the phone for personal use. It's just something that most people do and something that a lot of mothers and daughters do and perform as well. I am here to share with you, you must be extra careful with personal communication on the phone line as well. This is not always good and is not always a good practice of doing and performing.

Yes, mothers and daughters, others can come between your space even while you're on the phone, in and out through having a phone discussion. Protect your space and keep that space in and between your connection from within just because your inner vibration of your vibe you send it to the caller on the other end.

For this reason, you must be very wise and sharp at all times when communication is taking place with others for one simple fact. One could be really trying to bring you up under their control and power of influence, trying to cause an effect in an indirect or intangible way. This is why if you start feeling like you're being drained—guess what? You are getting drained, and the reason for the demented power exerting its influence is it is trying to bring you in and up under their weak, distorted control. But nevertheless, if you use space and keep your space, others will not be so lucky at playing you, as the young population likes to quote this word of use.

Now remember, manipulators are always trying to meet and trick someone who will come up under their will, and who will operate manually or mechanically in their influence of control. However, knowing the rules of space and practicing the art of space conversation, you will see it from within yourself in a very clear way. So, my beautiful mother of the world, let me make it a little more clear and just say it in a blunt way. Stop being used by the power of Satan's force to come up under that energy and motion to fall down in gossip. It is not something good for your daughter, or daughters, to keep seeing and witnessing their mother doing. Remember the caller on the other end doesn't care; they're just after one thing and thought, and that is to get what they want to attain, which is why you have to stand firm and strong in your own respected area of self and space. Otherwise, let the shore push my way through the games begin because guess what, that is what is going to be taken of place when space is not demanded.

Even animals demand space. This is a fact known throughout the animal kingdom. Even with pets in the home, cats and dogs will demand and desire that their space is given to them in the home as well. That's why sometimes when you have a cat in the home, you will miss your cat, and your cat will be nowhere to be found. That's because your cat is somewhere getting space. This is why a mother and daughter have to give each other space of respect.

Rest is also of respect. A mother can get her rest and not be interrupted, and the same can take place for the daughter when rest is needed for her as well. Also, when it's time for study, the daughter will be able to attain accurate information when she is studying. Most tasks of high importance will require space, knowing how to think and plan as well as executing well a fully carried out plan. This is what will help you to start feeling great and smart about yourself. A lot of people will talk so much about what they're going to do, and some will even write their plans out; but nevertheless, when it comes down to action, that is where so many people will drop the baton. And one of the main reasons is because it does take lots of strategy and a carefully worked out plan of action. You have to be very strategic in order to go into action. You must already see what your task of doing an accomplishment in your mind first is, then you can really work your way on into action. So with a mother and daughter keeping that space in their lives and in their living domain in and around them, strength will be gathered up and attained by both from within when they are ready to go straight into the fun of action.

Yes, action is and does become real fun when you keep hitting those mental home-run scores—what I like to call getting up and doing what you may want to with your beautiful life. However, it does require lots and lots of space, at the same time coupled with action. Yes, action—the motion of movement, which is what really does keep life spinning in much, much motion. Action is a very important word to us, but being it and doing it does require that space be kept between your heart from others. It will and does protect you from being and becoming dependent on others. We all need good space in our lives to create and do the things we really want to do in our lives, not to mention how important it really is for a mother and daughter to be on guard and have that guard of space of protecting and from protection from keeping others at their distance of where they're supposed to stay.

Let no one get in the way of your required work from yourself, mothers and daughters. Yes, I am going to say it very boldly—what I see happening a lot of times from mothers' and daughters' behavior, letting the male gender in and around to distract you from your work ethic or goals of satisfaction of accomplishment. As mothers and daughters, we really need to stop letting the male gender distract us from what would be done and needs to be done. You should not become weak to men.

Okay, I will admit a man can be sometimes very special to us—and special in so many fun and great ways—however, it's not good to become so weak in yourself due to another being. Don't do this to yourself and as well as to your beautiful future that's your guide for your life I am just going to be as 100 as I can to you from my point of view. From the wisdom realm, man can come and go. He can never promise himself to you, and if he does, I think he is clearly lying because deep down, he knows death can snatch him in a moment and at any second. Then what? Also, there's illness that can be a factor and take set and place in his life—then what? And not to mention, a man can just wake up and decide that being in your life is not what he wants to do, and he just downright doesn't want to ever see you again. Then what will you do? Will you be strong enough to just keep it moving, keep on pushing with your strong life? I hope so. Otherwise, falling down based around your life and lifestyle all revolved around someone else's life orbit will make it very difficult and of much challenge to get back up and take strong control over your life.

This why, mothers and daughters, you cannot allow anyone to come in and take you down so much until they're starting and getting away at tripping you up and tearing you down. Trust me when I share this bold statement. People will do this. If and when a man does it, he will seriously knock you down. So, mothers and daughters, don't take your life for granted. Set those everyday goals and really give it all your power and might to accomplish those goals. You will start to feel real good and very excellently about yourself, which is a good thing. There is nothing like making a strong and good effort at doing and achieving what you set your mind out to do and accomplish. You will start to grow into the art of having respect for defense without honor for having respect for defense, Man will come into your life and basically step right on you and won't care at all. Guard your space. Have respect for your space so you can see what others really want from you. Remember, you want to really be able to see the play-play hat that they're wearing.

Remember that what others like to communicate with you, it does not necessarily mean it's true, and how their feelings are toward you. People play so many mind games; however, if your learn how to stay in your own beautiful mind, you will be able to see it and recognize it. Otherwise, if you allow others to take you out of your own mind and cause you to get all caught up out of your own space and into theirs, the game of control will begin. Those that are for real, like yourself, will not and do not want to trip you down in order to gain control over yourself and your lifestyle, which brings me back to sharing why space between a mother and daughter is just so much of extra importance. Having this space allows a mother and daughter to have respect for each other, being very much aware as to why others must give you your space.

Now, mothers and daughters, remember there are folks out there who just straight out and downright do not really give 1 percent about you having that space that you do need in order to practice good, clear thinking and do of good service in your everyday life. And these energy drainers are looking from every angle to come at you to bring your mental strength to zero, just to see and watch that you come up under their control of influence of manipulation and do believe a person does know when you're under their control and you start behaving mechanically like their own personal robot. Sometimes we can and will think of others, not knowing what's really taking place from their behavior or what they're doing. Most do know what they're doing; they just do not care as long as their job of manipulation is being performed and practiced on you. However, you can stop this just by keeping space. Then you will most certainly see what's really taking place.

Where there is no space, trust me when I say you're going to see how problems do get started. Mothers and daughters, watch and observe closely when others try to get next to you—get close by you to bring you from your connection from your spirit to operate you under flesh control. All I am saying is watch out close and look at what's taking place because you really don't know what their hidden agenda is and guess what others don't have to tell you. However, if you are really watching closely, you will see it for yourself. That's why one of those number 1 rules in your home has to be "Give one another space." Your outcome will always be much better for you in your life.

This is why the word *cousin* can really be defined as because of the distance sometimes, a cousin can seem so far away. However, at the same time, a cousin can live ten minutes away; however, space will determine the ones whom you have more likes about of sharing things with and situations in common, whereas those loved ones as of nothing in common with. I think it's always a real good thing to keep that space—otherwise, it won't take too long for confrontation. And it will begin. Even when a mother teaches her daughter how to clean up correctly and wash clothes, there is a way to do a thing in a correct way or manner.

Space is a must; reason for information must be processed correctly when given out to someone in a teaching manner. If you use your energy in a rude way, pushing too far and over on the student (in this case, your daughter), the information that you're given will not be received correctly. So therefore, problems are going to occur just because the code of notation of space has entered, which is and only is going to throw everything off balance. And so therefore, no one wins—the mother or the daughter. The mother loses because of not gaining her trust from her daughter of being able to allow her mom to practice teaching skills; and the daughter loses because she does not get the information that she needs in order to further her learning and developmental skills!

I will quote the magic formula once again. Space is really of much need between a mother and daughter. As needed, we all should want happy results in our home. Why have distorted and confused energy in and around your place of residence, which can stem from not having and keeping space? Now do and always remember, sometimes others will get upset when they are able to see and recognize that you have set strong, solid, and firm boundaries that you have revolved around keeping space that distance. However, that's their problem and confusion of their owning in and of their tripped-up life and lifestyle, not yours. Always remember the rules and the way we all should want in front of our lives and that we should live by. However, some just don't care and don't respect solid rules. So therefore, that's why the art of space must be applied and practiced.

In bringing in my final conclusion of "The Rules of Space between a Mother and Daughter," let no one rob you of your gift that we all have, and that is greatly cherished of valued precious time of use every day in life and standing up for your power of rule of given space. Peace.

The Respect that Goes between a Mother-Daughter Bond

What is this word *respect* really all about? Is it really true what people like to share? Have respect for yourself, and it will take you long and far on a good, long journey in your own ownership of your beautiful life. Yes, it is all about that golden word *respect*, which is why the center of the respect goes a long way through and must be at the center of a mother-and-daughter bond in their relationship of unity. A really true and good mother knows that her relationship with her daughter does have to be built around solid trust. When their relationship is built around solid trust and respect, they're very much able to enter into so many portal entrances that a mother and daughter can take and go, and so much of the great and good rewards will be given to them both. Just because of respect, that aura of respect will be present and around them both.

Let's just face it—what I call just being real. When a mother and daughter have respect for themselves, their presence together is much bold when out in the world with of its inhabitants sometime to others of viewing this respect of their seeing can be of pleasant to the onlooker, or in some cases, very intimidating. Remember, sometimes unity does really make some people very much of being nervous just because lacking and having respect for themselves, and sometimes not having respect for their own mother can and will cause the eyes of red anger to pop through and try to look down on that respect that's of showing and of witness right staring back at through their eyes of bloodshot red deep from within.

We all know that a mother should be held with a high regard of respect. I mean, for real. Really think about it. Your mother is the one who has brought you down into the world we all live in, which is why it is just so right when you see that respect that goes between a mother-and-daughter bond. There is no one in the world who did not come through their mother; however, I know in some cases from doing research, some really do complain about having certain issues with regard to what kind and type of mother that they're of having, and I always like to quote for this reason that no one is really perfect. We can be of good practice, but all will make mistakes. So yes, a strong mother-daughter relationship will and can have a strong effect on you, because a mother truly does have to teach her daughter, or daughters, that standing up for yourself is truly a must. Without a strong stance in your life, people will try to show up and knock you right out of it; however, you do not have to allow this to happen if you keep practicing the art of staying in your stance. When I say staying in your stance, I mean staying firm in what it is you have to do and not letting anyone set up blocks to run in with the energy of distractions. If you're not dedicated at what you tell your inner self that you must do and accomplish others well since that their able to break in and through your structure and what structure starts with is yourself and that's who will be the breakdown target.

A real mom knows she is an asset to her daughter as well when a mother teaches this to her at a young age. I see so many young females getting dogged out and used by young males taking over total control of a car that the young girl purchased from her own money—purchase from her own good high credit score, her own proof of income. Her purchase of her car had totally nothing to do with this male of a kind user, and when it comes straight down to it, you will let a bully take your car keys when he wants to! Wake up, young girls! This is not a young man in your presence. This is a taker—a bully! Do you even know what a bully is? Most people know a bully as someone who intimidates others; however, most people leave out that a bully also is one who hurts you. Any real mother would not want to see her daughter hurt, and a daughter who truly, really does respect herself will not allow someone to bully her around and take from her what does belong to her.

Young girls who find themselves in present situations as this one must wake up. This is very dangerous. And don't think that this is someone who cares a lot about you, or who loves you. Just think for a minute. It's really not a sin to think. Put your thinking cap on. If you where smart enough to figure out and calculate how to purchase your own car, you can do math to some degree. So I know you can add it up and see that you are getting used and taken advantage of in a bold way. Remember, daughter, you really do have to learn and see yourself as an asset. You are higher than material items and objects. Don't allow and let anyone use up the material items that you worked hard to get and attain, and for certain, stop letting others use you up. Your beautiful self is a given gift from the Creator. You: yourself. It's time to wake up and look and really view what's going on and taking place in and around you and your life every day. Otherwise, the big bad wolf is ready to come and take you down and leave you in a zero state of mind, not giving one cent of care about you. Remember, in the realm of power, power don't care if you huff and puff—all it is hoping for is that you huff and puff and tire yourself right on out, just in order to receive the victory and be the real winner.

Mothers, keep respecting yourselves and keep teaching respect for your daughter and daughters. There is that old saying that will really always be brand-new: respect will take you many far places in life if you keep it at the front of your life and not second-guess it. I found this to be very true. It's free to make some effort to live by it. Remember, respect and morals are not things people can purchase from you; respect and morals come from within and you holding stern to your beliefs and of what's important to you and what principle foundation you stand on. Remember, you must make an extra-strong effort to keep the rain off you, and this comes from you not forgetting to carry your own umbrella, which is a device to protect you from the sun or rain. So, basically, what I am sharing and have given you is a clear perception what an umbrella is for. Bottom line: your respect and your morals of structure are your own devices of protection when you don't second-guess yourself. When you start second-guessing yourself and others pick up on a vibration of you not really thinking or caring too much about yourself, they're going to see you for a merry-go-round on the playing field at the park, which is why you should be very bold and straightforward about who you are and what you stand for. It only keeps you in the seat of respect and winning in your own special life.

Every day, a mother and daughter must get up with the glow of respect and keep respecting themselves. It also starts with protecting your creative energy, and when I say creative energy, do not allow others to stretch you into what they want you to do without thinking about it first. And at the same time, use clear viewing to see what it is you should be doing the reason why you cannot afford your own time of importance to get locked up, caught up tied down in others problems and complaints of others weak thought out plans in their lives and life styles of others problems that others sometime live in! When a mother and daughter do not monitor their energy other's will try to bring in their distorted energy if you allow it remember it is okay to pick up the stop sign. Some things you just don't go on, and you most certainly don't just yield as well. This is why I do believe true teamwork does start in a mother-and-daughter relationship; good team playing does start in the home with whom we see and live around every day in our lives. So this is why it's very important to be made very aware that not all others care and take entrance and delight, and are fascinated by you winning and of the best gains for your life. A high percentage could really care less, and there is that somewhat small percentage that may care—however, if you don't know how to keep caring about your own self, it will be hard to recognize the ones that do care!

So, mothers and daughters, stay focused and inspired to love your own self and look out for your own well-being. When thinking from the mental realm of respect, you will look from a closer range. When it comes to your actions and deeds, remember there are those out there who will hunt you down just because of viewing and seeing your self-worth and self-respect as a challenge. However in your own personal reality you're not a challenge to anyone. It is all about keeping your own challenge of yourself and for yourself in your life every day.

But from those who see life as another dragging day and are just out to see if they are able to distract someone off their path or feel as if they having nothing to do if you allow it their energy will be able to distract you off your path feeling as you're their challenge, which I am here to say keep these distracter individuals out in the streets where they belong their nothing but serious problems as I write now and well as later on in all you beautiful mothers' and daughters' lives, when reasoning and logic thinking starts deviating from a mother and daughter their sound thinking problems will start accruing you will have opened portals for others lifestyles of hell and confusion that their life and lifestyle of a problem vortex is in and spinning around in their lives will come in yours, which is why keeping your own center of respect for yourself will keep reasoning and logic at the front of a mother's and daughter's thinking. Others' confusion will just have to bounce right off because you will not only have any time to give to the art of foolish behavior. But nevertheless, you will not want to participate with foolishness as well.

Respect helps you really gain control over all areas of your self as well as to how you live your life and conduct yourself. Remember others don't care about you as much as you want them to. You have to be and become extra responsible for caring about your own self. The more you start caring strongly about yourself and all your daily duties, carrying out your action plans, a level of high respect will get stronger for a mother with her daughter just because of moving around in having an aura of respect. Things of accomplishment will manifest and appear close and near in your life. This will only cause a daughter to think more happy thoughts with regard to her mother. Remember, carrying high regards can and really will change your life and lifestyle for the best; however, in order for happy results to be of good comment for a mother's and daughter's lives, your thinking thoughts must be positive. Otherwise, negative self-doubts will creep in, and that will only lead and cause a mother and daughter to lose their own special mirror, and self-hate will get in. Remember, we all have a mirror in our lives that is of much requirement to be looked in and viewed from within ourselves every day. The big problems start occurring when we stop and don't take the time to really look inside our mirror.

Every mother and daughter is given the gift of imagination and to have respect for each one and only themselves. It's a daily responsibility to keep at it and maintain self-respect. As mothers and daughters, we must keep at it. The art of practicing good, positive self-talk as well at the same time keeping hope alive in life's situations and circumstances that we can encounter at certain times even if these events are not divine planning you will still be able to be rewarded with having boldness and the audacity to keep hoping and keep hope alive! When a mother and daughter really do keep at hoping to bring better changes in their lives, things will and can only really be only one way and that is to just really too get much better.

Mothers and daughters, we must keep striving every day of our lives of excellence and respect. Remember, in life, it is about aiming to win in our lives and lifestyles; rather we win are not still winning should really be are aim, mothers and daughters! You will feel so much better inside yourself when you know how much you must you must strive to be a better person in society. The things of importance will start to manifest more crystal-ball clear for you, and you will really become so strong at not wasting your time as well as wasting others' time. However, at the same time, you will have no tolerance for others to come into your life and waste your time. This is why the word *respect* is so strong and a powerful word. When you start really respecting yourself, it goes much further than just the word as mother and for a daughter as well. Your actions and motion of how you carry yourself and the way you get things done all revolve around the center of you respecting your actions and deeds.

People tend to want to misjudge and, oftentimes, may want to take part and participate in communicating a lot of unworthy conversation about you. However, mothers and daughters, you keep on moving right along in motion of progress and action. Keep it moving right along with your action plan and good, positive behavior. Others will always be around, but you must really know that if you stop and don't take care of yourself, you will be the one to blame. Remember, there are just no grand limits to living a good, successful, and rewarding life. You can do it! Just keep moving right along and do best at what you are best at, and that really should be to keep on loving yourself. Self is always present when everything else changes and leaves. And yes, so many people really don't care as much as you think, which is why the main goal is for you to care about your own personal well-being.

Mothers and daughters, take extra excellent care of yourself. This is very strong teamwork between a mother and daughter staying very much focused and so self-centered around each of you, your own life. I sometimes like and enjoy hearing our younger generation's discussions, saying, "I am going to do me, and you go do you." Otherwise, what's really being of sharing is I am going to look after self and take strong, good care of myself regardless. If you take care of your own self, which is very important words do you know why? Because doing you is really so much fun, and to be of real, true honesty, it really is your own personal responsibility. However, let no one else make you really think of much difference, keeping respect at the hard core and at the front and the center of your life, things will only but manifest the way you really want them to.

When a mother and daughter keep that divine respect in front of their lives, they're able to make so much more manifest than what would accrue and happen for them. Both know and really do understand that they're a team of power, having respect in this high regard for themselves only. It keeps a mother and daughter in strong unity. A real mother will not drain her daughter's energy, and a real and true loving daughter will not drain her mother as well, because they both understand what's happening, mostly from other people. Most really do want to try and get in your life and drain you if feeling as though of being able to just get away with doing so which is nothing but a totally no respect rhythm of a pull-you-down motion.

Mothers and daughters of beauty and strength, hold your heads up high and just straight up. Do not allow this to happen and take place in and around yourselves and as well as in your life and on your life. Remember, you really do have to remain and have serious control over you own life, every day and every second of your life. A mother and daughter must become a powerful team every day in their life how as too having too being a rhythm of persistence, meaning really go on resolutely in spite of whatever difficulties that may continue to exist in front and all around their beautiful life. Strong respect—in very, very high regards—must be so strong and firm in all areas of their daily chores and activities throughout how living life is centered. At times, there can be such a high battle in regard to deep down from within our soul and spirit of how to really keep respect at the center of us and all around.

There are so many times in our lives we can experience others who will try to fake their way closer in and around us to just see if we really respect ourselves as much as we say so. Remember, every day in your beautiful life can really be a serious test just to see how much we do really care and respect our own presence. Sometimes things, people, and certain situations will happen and really occur just to see how much self-control and self-respect one really does have. Yes, this is and can be a real inner battle at times just because you have so many people who come up to you and say this and that. However, you have to have such a high regard and high respect for yourself that you won't get tripped up in really what is nothing but other people's play-play hats and the way a mother and daughter keep others' play-play hats off their own head. Your own crown is by doing what you should be doing every moment, every second, in their own life being real to yourself and chasing yourself every day in a good and wise manner of what you should really be doing. This will clear your divine path of your aura of respect to be and stay around you. This respect from a mother to her daughter will only cause her to keep challenging her daughter to be all that she can be and to do her very best at keeping and giving herself a great chance at living her life in a good way to her fullest, highest potential every day.

Every day, a mother and daughter must really compete and challenge themselves to keep and demand that honor of respect around themselves, and being and having respect does and will require you to be so much of a smart person just because you really do have to think as well and really start thinking even more, because sometimes we think of something or a situation as what we want it to be. However, it can and may not even be of that; so therefore, I like to use the famous word are brain then we just have to accept the facts and keep it moving on and on in a divine and respectful way.

I like to just call it all what it really is. It's just our beautiful lives with its curve balls that are sometimes thrown our way, and we mess up and try to catch a curve ball from a straight angle, and we miss it. This is why so much respect is giving and really do must be seriously at the front of a mother-and-daughter relationship. Having and keeping strong respect really will and really does unlock and open the pearly gates of heaven on physical earth. You seek the right way, so therefore, you should really find true peace and real happiness. I just have to speak it: the opposite of peace is war. The way I see it, war is really straight up hell, the same for being confused. There is just no way you can really get things and situations really taken care of when there is no respect for yourself. All that will happen and seriously take place is serious confusion. All that confusion does is start up a bunch of mental stabs toward who you are yourself your good productive being of who you are not a good energy you want to operate in this is a energy that you want void give it know serious force and purpose and aim at having excess toward your rubies, diamonds, emeralds, and pearls within yourself. Bottom line, beautiful mothers and daughters: your self is what should be of your most concern of your being, and that comes from really deep from within and starts from having and keeping serious self-control over you always, which is why self-respect is a number-one priority in a mother and daughter's life. Having this respect will keep your life and lifestyle in so much high regards of high respect, not to mention just so many different routes to how the golden rules of respect will open and lead a mother and daughter toward and to so many ways of enjoyment for their lives and, at the same time, carrying and maintaining a dignity of self-respect and self-control.

A mother must make sure she always teaches her daughter to carry herself in a very respectful way and manner of poise. This good behavior will only make it more simple from an onlooker's view to see and know that boundaries are all around you. When boundaries are really set, it lets off a strong, serious energy vibe that a high force field of self-protection is really around. I am a true believer that without serious, meaningful business boundaries, you start to fall for whatever does come your way, and you most certainly will lose control over your lives, mothers and daughters. Don't let Satan—that force of evil—have victory over your life and all your divine goals and plans for your lives. Mothers and daughters, we really do have to know how to defeat our enemies and our wrongful opponent. You know who I am talking about.

Let me just make it more plain and real in a very clear angle those distracting ones, which can be males or females, and yes, I will say those so-called family members who really are supposed to be in our corners and have our backs but, nevertheless, are just as rotten as a place of hellfire burning in their eyes to just come right in and distract and take away at our everyday progress if and when allowing their wrong, crazy takedown energy behavior into our lives. I say it's really time, mothers and daughters, to pick up your mighty swords of truth and take serious control and ownership over your own beautiful lives, and let no one pull you and drag your lifestyle and mind into a dirty pit of thinking in a realm of low self-esteem, which only in the long run will produce a rutlike energy of no motion, not being able to do the things you really want to and accomplish every day and prevention of going places of being and attending events of importance. This is why it's just so important for mothers and daughters too stand up in respect together. It's time to really get up, stand up, and think in a mathematical way. When I speak on thinking in a mathematical way, we must not tolerate foolish behavior that wants to get its way into our beautiful lives. We really don't have time and room for unnecessary dust thinking in our lives—dusting thinking really does not do us all any good and really doesn't serve any divine purpose at all.

A mother and daughter must really be able to stand up together and think together in a right, smart, good old-fashioned, common-sense way to make good things happen in their lives, as well as bring good things and good events into their lives and not to mention be of good deeds and of good services to help others. It is so and very amazing how people can really see clearly and view the respect when seeing the energy of respect between a mother and daughter. People will never be or become blind to how the respect of divine order looks and its mannerism and behavior deep from within. We all know that it does take divine order and a strong structure of bonding from within to really get things done and moving. The more we live, the more we see living life as a precious gift. There is just no room and tolerance for the bond breakdown that really only stems from energy and motion pertaining to confusion and self–hate. You don't want it in your life, and there really is no gain from participating in this rhythm. So yes—I, Roshaunda, do agree there really should be a movement pertaining to the proper respect that is between mothers and daughters in and all around the world.

I have heard so many stories about how outside individuals will come into a mother and daughter's home and seriously break away at tearing away the bond if of viewing it as weak or in a sense that their of convinced that mother and daughter just argue and in some cases fight, which is really bad. And if fighting does take place between mothers and daughters, this rotten and bad behavior is a serious and dirty problem, which something really did happen in the early stages of their lives. As a team, it is just not to be respected to see a mother and daughter fighting. Now I did not say a mother disciplining her daughter know discipline and guidance is totaling something different. A mother disciplines her daughter just out of caring, and no matter what age her daughter reaches, she will always pay attention to where she goes and what she does; however, she does not try to control her or control her life, but peek in and watch with really good intent, all under the law of caring.

When a mom has a good, healthy, solid bond with her daughter, she really does know how far to take it, how far to go. Now I will speak out about being against a mother trying to take over her daughter's lifestyle and trying to control her choices and dissensions. It's okay to point out and make valued good, sound advice. I think we all can benefit from good advice. Good-advice behavior is okay; it's when you take it too far. Besides, it's your daughter's life, and she is the one who has to live in her own skin and move around in her own motion, which is why she is the one who really does have to be comfortable with what she agrees to take action on.

Always remember that real respect is always present in the centerpiece when you enter into a situation, performing it the right, proper, and correct way. A lot of times, people will really forfeit respect being the centerpiece anyway, just because of bad behavior. And yes, there are mothers in this world who are totally doing it wrong when it comes to teaching and giving the right, sound advice to their daughter or daughters. I know this really is a very scary and serious subject to discuss because so many mothers will speak out with a rough and hard tone: "This is my daughter (or daughters), and no one tells me what to do and say to them!" I know they're your daughters; however, it's really bad to keep doing something wrong over and over when it's only going to keep getting worse and worse.

Let's just be real within and with ourselves. No one is perfect, and we all—from time to time—need some correction. Now, for some, it's only a little—however, for others, it's a whole lot of correction. Most people cringe when something is pointed out to them, while others may laugh out loud and not take it that seriously, while on the other end, you have others who accept the truth and will say "ouch" and admit to needing divine help, and it's of showing up to get their medicine. Yes, there is a science dealing in the realm of truth and getting something right and corrected. It's almost in the same fashion when you go to the doctor to get checked out. And of course, if the doctor does tell you something is wrong, we sometimes have to take the pain and get what it is we may need in order to help us feel better. Trust what I am saying: no one wants to be written off as just plain bad off their are choices in life, and I think that no one should fall down in the tunnel of hell being bad off due to not being able to accept and take correction. Just own up to it; we all can use a little help sometimes. I didn't say all the time however most certainly sometime this is just hard plain facts that we all have to admit and just get straight used to it.

We all must admit that the truth does ruffle you up, and I know sometimes mothers and daughters can battle to keep that realm of high respect in and around their connection of their mother-daughter bond relationship. However, the glue to keeping that connection, that respect, must be their respect is something that cannot really be faked, or made out like it's of your having and you don't. It will seriously expose you straight—bring you out and expose your lack of respect and understanding.

From doing research, I have witnessed with my own eyes that some mothers and daughters really do not have any understanding of even knowing that respect and honor should be the center of a mother's relationship with her daughter, or her daughters, which is why so much have a lack of knowledge with understanding. You really will perish operating in the realm of not knowing. I heard so many individuals say this; and yes, it is so true. When you don't know a thing or two about something, trying to operate from not knowing it is only going to trip your own motion up and seriously take you down in strong confusion. My conclusion of this chapter—"The Respect that Goes between a Mother-Daughter Bond"—starts first with your own self-worth, and there will be no doubt as to having and keeping respect as the center for a mother-daughter bond.

A Mother's Real Love for a Daughter

Let's discuss the real value of a mother's love for her daughter. I can start out by saying a real mother wants the super best for her daughter, and that sometimes can mean to excel to do extremely well, far better than her. Sometimes, as mothers, we will admit later on in life if—or had I done it this way, or took a turn that way—my lifestyle would have reached a better stance. Which is why, as a good mother, we will extend, stretch forth outward, and share our hidden mistakes and secrets with our daughter and hope for the best, that she listens carefully and that the mistakes a mother can make can be an example for a daughter's view to take in and go for her dreams, as well as attain those dreams and bring them into fruition or completion.

When a mother loves her daughter from a right way of the mother-daughter bond, she does not fall down into gossip and bad judgment of her daughter. A real mom knows no one is perfect. A wise mother does not gossip about her daughter's flaws with other people, and the same goes for bragging and boasting. A real mother does no such thing. She knows all this spells out is trouble, and it is a doorway for confusion to enter into her mind and turn her mother-daughter bond into disrespect and corruption—which is not a good behavior, not a bond of love. However, this is how the bond of hate will get in and seriously destroy a mother's real love from within, which is why a real mother is just not going there with you. She is not going to involve herself in that wrong behavior.

I really do believe if more women would bond in love the right way with their daughters, there would be a stronger connection when it comes to team leadership of women committed to working together.

I am in no way saying women don't work together or aren't coming together to get things done and make a stance of importance for what their strong beliefs are; however, a high percentage don't from my field of doing research. I truly believe it has a lot to do with real love bonding that comes from a mother who has that genuine bond that she gives to her daughter. The real bond of love will restrict you from the realm of so much unnecessary gossip that a high percentage women partake in from notice and observation. Some are so pulled into it and are really not aware as to how to not allow that going-nowhere, out-of-control energy in.

I give you an example. View Michelle Obama in your mind and eyes. When viewing her, you will think twice about trying to pull her into gossip and confusion. Her bond of love is sitting right in her heart, her genuine seat of love you can just see clearly. She did not fall down into a fake belief of no self-worth. She had the proper bond of love from her mother, which is why she can and does know how to return it and give it to her two beautiful daughters.

Proper and right bonding is a very powerful and good force. It will always alert you when something is not going right and when you should back away from certain people and situations that are getting close to you and to your heart. Sometimes it's sort of hard for us, as humans, to really admit it and accept that with some people, you really do have to keep them at a near distance; otherwise, if you don't, they are going to bring in so many unnecessary problems just because their bond within themselves is seriously off balance, like a rocket tilted and ready to skyrocket up and blast on you all their garbage of negativity. This is why it's so important that a mother does bond the right way with her daughter.

Share words of positive encouragement with your daughter. Don't put and instill fear and despair energy on your daughter. You want to impart and, in a gradual process, help your daughter or daughters in some matters to grow and bloom into beautiful flowers. Just imagine if flowers received no water! When you give your flowers no water and care, what will happen is they are going to die off. It's the same concept with our daughters. Mothers, you must help them—build your daughter up. Stop tearing away at their self-esteem. Life, in general, will try to have people cross your path and try to tear at you anyway—which is why, mothers, you really don't want your daughter to view you as those same-spirited individuals that I like to call the "knock you down, tear you down" ones.

A good strong mother who knows love is the answer, and that how Love heals you and brings you into soundness and wholeness. What a great joy and such a beautiful reward that comes from a mother. Your daughter is a gift of love given by the Creator from heaven, the realm up above that comes down and somehow finds you, and they're in your life.

I'know sometimes, as women, we can find our lives in such circumstances or have had to encounter unwanted events, only to find out that these events that have happened may have only caused us pain. And sometimes not wanted inner stab aches scars of serious memory pain. And sometimes we birth our daughters from men who may have hit us—not receiving the proper, right, good attention from them—and only to find out we were getting abused all around that situation. But your daughter comes into the world, or your daughters. Rejoice, your blessing is here, so don't let that bad rotten apple ruin your joy. You're supposed to help.

Mothers, show real love to your daughter and take the time to help her become what she should become. As mothers, we really must break these bad, nasty patterns of tearing down and taking our daughter's self-esteem to zero. When you do this, getting it back is tripple hard—not to kick at you, but it's going to kick you straight in your face. And I know this is not what you want. No one wants to get kicked in the face, and no one certainly deserves to be kicked in the face. What I am sharing is karma. It is very real, and what we do to others, in some way, will come back to us. So you see, mothers, you really do have to love and own up to proper respect and responsibility for taking good care of yourself and loving yourself every day so you can have it to give.

As mothers, we must value ourselves more, value our time more. Stop gossiping in the streets about our daughters' business. Learn to value your "for me" time and guess what you really will come into: strength to protect yourself from BS and drain-down energy. You will grow stronger in knowing how to have what I like to call "keep it pushing" energy, because if you don't grow into the energy and keep it pushing, keep it moving, keep it growing—I am going to say it plain and clear. You are going to stop growing, and your mind is going to start rotting and decay out those filthy thoughts, which only lead to filthy deeds of actions; and I do believe this is why, sometimes, it is such a struggle for a mother to show real strong love to her daughter. Sometimes, when you are out of your home, if you're not watchful or careful, you can gather lots of others' negative thinking. It will and can corrupt your own self-bonding of good, which causes a bad root to come in, and you will pass it on and down into your bond with your daughter.

It is not a good thing; you don't want this to happen. You want a good, loving, healthy bond of real happy love sent down and through you from our Almighty Creator. What you don't want to experience is that bond of hell of confusion bringing and what I call out to be tearing your daughter down. You want a positive bond with your daughter. Remember, positive energy produces a positive lifestyle; and as mothers, this is why we want to remain responsible, showing and carrying so much for our daughters that deep from within our hearts, we want better for them than ourselves. If all it is from us of given encouragement and that we are, then this is what is mandatory of us. It's not good for a daughter to go through being starved of proper caring from her mom.

There are so many unwanted, hidden curveballs that negative ones with low self-esteem will try and throw at you, and when you're not clear as to what it is, you can sometimes think that you may have to catch the baggage ball of others—and you truly, really don't have to catch negativity when it is thrown your way.

Mothers, we can stop a lot of this foolish behavior from entering our homes just by showing the proper love in a household where there is a lot of screaming and yelling, and you're doing this toward your daughter. This is really the wrong way to get the right motion going— when you scream and yell and you think this is what should be done in order to make things and situations go right. It will only make it all worse. Remember, love is like a welcome door that opens with a good fragrant smell. Love means so much enjoyment in life, and as mothers, you should want your daughter to take in all the joy and as much joy as they are able to do so. Which is why having control over how energy is used and is going out is very important. You will grow at becoming a better decision maker, which is something that is very important in a mother's life as well as of importance for a mother to help and guide her daughter into making wise choices and decisions.

A real mother knows she must teach and show her daughter how to really make sound, logical, good choices for her life; and that can really start at such a young age when a mom notices that her daughter is about to leave the house without a jacket or sweater and she knows that it is really cold outside. She will share with her daughter right then, "Get your coat." At that stage in her daughter's life, she is showing her right. Then the power of the right choice or choices in your life will only make it so much easier and better for you, as long as you keep observation around your own life and keep practicing the art of making the best choice for your life and all those events that will somehow surface in and around your life.

When a mom loves her daughter, she is going to do her best to not only just tell her daughter to get a good education, she is also going to do everything in her power to show her the process as well, because she knows that education is a path and a process in life that everyone should always stay on. Learning is something we do every day and as well not allow anyone to come between your learning capability. Knowing how to process information and knowing what to do in any given situation is of so much real importance. It could save your life, or your life could really depend on what you do at that moment. So the love a mom has for her daughter is for her to tell her daughter to always think smart, be smart, and do smart as well.

A mother is always sharing with her daughter regarding how there will be things and situations that will sometimes come into your life and find a way at challenging your thinking, your choices, and your decision making. And this will require you to be smart and have quick right thinking, and you must really know what to do and say. It will all depend just on you and from no one else in life, which does require you to really be ready, and your takeoff must be right and seriously ready for go, like going on that green light—no time for yield or pause. Just go when it's time to move on action remember stop is not the time. Just imagine all those cars going at a fast space on your local freeway, and if a few cars just decided to just stop, this would be a very dumb decision and, not to mention, a really bad choice, causing bad accidents that lead to so much danger. So being a real good mother and showing real love of real and pure heartfelt caring does make a big difference when going out into the big beautiful world we all live in and have to move and go through it on an everyday basis.

Most of us have heard that saying how a mother's job is never done and how a mother always has that stinger on her back. I find these sayings to be so truthful just because real love is giving so much, and really caring so much as well as feeling so much is rewarded in the areas of doing and saying what must be said and done. A mother is always teaching, giving, and showing. A mother knows that she must be very responsible for showing and doing what must and has to be done. This behavior only grows real trust and respect from her daughter, which only will stretch her daughter's energy into being that of a better listener and of being a more cautious listener when being spoken to inside the home as well as outside the home. Also, the way a mom will demonstrate her love for her daughter is by telling and sharing some of the mistakes she made throughout her life. A mother knows there is a lot of real value in sharing about those mistakes with her daughter. She is also aware of how sometimes a daughter really can learn from her mom with regard to what may not be in her best interests to do certain such things. A mother's real love for her can be considered tough love; however, your life can be tough as well, so this is why a real mother is going to do whatever it takes for her to instill the inherited real strong, good values in her daughter's life.

A mom knows there are so many people in the world who are really always wearing their joker hats—not just one joker hat but many different kinds of joker hats—and if you're not watching closely, the joker card will be played on you and as well played in and all through and around your lifestyle. There are so many things and situations that are done by so many women when reaching a higher age that is totally wrong, and in the long run, all it is and will do for certain is bring so much, and such shame to your life and on you as a person, which most of these bad-behavior lifestyles really could have been null and void had Mom told us what could and would happen because of such not-so-good behavior or in some given situations. Mom may have shared a few good words of advice, and her daughter or daughters may just have not listened and, as a result of not listening, caused bad and wrong behavior to make a manifestation to happen, causing all the wrong results. This is why it is very important for a mom to teach her daughter good listening skills at a very young age. When this is taught at a very young age, the more her daughter starts to mature. She will still have the respect of listening. This is why screaming and yelling all throughout your house is not the best behavior to practice.

Now I am not saying not to speak and communicate with authority—however, there is a good way of getting your words out besides showing no self-control by yelling and screaming. You can speak in a commanding tone of being serious, and you will be taken as very serious and being someone who is not playing games, who means what she is saying. This is why when you are outside your home or maybe in the shopping mall, and if you hear two people screaming and yelling at each other, all who see this behavior are going to turn around and view this behavior as if something is going on and that something is wrong. Most likely, security will be called and will show up and tell you in a serious way that this must stop. And if it does not, you will be escorted by security to leave right now. However, if you keep at acting this way, handcuffs are put on the out-of-control ones, and this leads to the station, which means they are taken to jail.

I said all this to point out that if screaming and yelling is wrong in public, then it most certainly is wrong in the home with our daughters. When you are the authority in your home, you think it's okay because security is not there to tell you of how out-of-control you are behaving. I am not badmouthing or pointing the finger. I am just saying it's still free to think about what we do and say, so why not take it for granted? It is still a free right. We are charged for water and now paper bags. Thinking is still free. Let's keep on thinking while it's still a free thing to do. So it's a joke; however, I am saying it in a joking way. However, most will admit to not seeing the charge of ten cents for paper bags.

So, mothers, we must stay on top of our game that we orchestrate in our lives every single day. Yes, every day—not every other day. We must arrange for best effect and best results for our daughters being not just our daughters but, however, ourselves—as we must have self-love for ourselves. In order to give it out to our daughters, we must begin to know that it is really okay to wake up in the morning and say those positive affirmations that "I love myself" and that "I will even grow more each and every day, loving like the Creator has recommended for me to be." When a daughter sees this beautiful kind of energy flowing and growing through the home that she lives and resides in, it only brings her self-esteem up twice as much.

It's all about sharing and expressing positive energy. Real love is almost like being a demonstration of that smell of fresh homemade apple pie being baked when you walk into the house. You can smell the aroma of apple pie as soon as you get to your front kitchen door. What a good smell, and it gets even twice as good once you slice it and taste it and the aftertaste of finishing it. It just keeps on getting better and better, which is a comparison of how a mother's love for her daughter grows and grows, blooming her life and lifestyle into a blossom of joy.

Real love in all and any divine situations is like a golden key that unlocks the difficult doors in life. Sometimes there are just so many hard-to-do and difficult things and situations that really are not easy to understand or easy to manage and deal with. However, sometimes, through the power of love, we somehow will manage to use our key of love and guess what the door really does unlock and open for us. So you see, in all our getting, we have to use love as well as the understanding of all in a dynamic relating physical force that produces the motion of that energetic or forceful powerful motion that sometimes really makes us just do right. The more the skill of doing right becomes more of a daily reality for a mom and daughter, the more both are really able to set forth and really make it happen and produce the kind of reality that's needed for the path of success to keep on at its highest level of manifestation.

Appear and show up. Yes, I am talking about showing up. As mothers, we must teach our daughters the power of showing up to take care of business, as well as to make sure what should be done is taken care of. Then we can move on to what's next and what's of right behavior and, most certainly, of how to know what's not right and to see wrong. As mothers, once you have mastered that truly fine art of showing your daughter right from wrong and you can see from her conduct and behavior that she does now know right from wrong—guess what, Mother? You have now done your job, and that is truly the art of love that a mother has for her daughter.

Much love and respect,

Roshaunda Alexander
Butterfly Love

What I hope to *teach* you

What it is you are *great* at

Certain is it that
there is no kind of affection
so purely angelic as of a father
to a daughter. In love to our wives
there is desire; to our sons, ambition;
but to our daughters, there is
something which there are
no words to express.
—Joseph Addison

funny things

Things I hope
you never
forget

CPSIA information can be obtained
at www.ICGtesting.com
Printed in the USA
LVHW090933201220
674414LV00008B/670